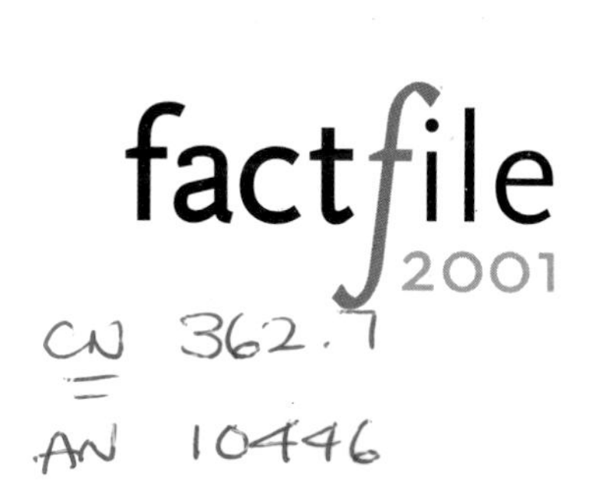

F

cl

NCH

ISBN 0 900984 70 8

Produced by NCH

Printed by Chapel Press, Rochester, Kent

Introduction

Welcome to *FactFile 2001*. *FactFile* is NCH's annual compendium of key facts and statistics about Britain's children. Regular readers will notice the new handy pocket-sized format.

In keeping with the times, we are delighted to announce that from 2002, *FactFile* will be published on our website (www.nch.org.uk). Any future text versions will be in summary form only. Our website will also set out information about the public policy issues affecting children and NCH's views about them.

We hope you will agree that 'less is more' so far as *FactFile 2001* is concerned, and that you will find it to be an easily accessible source of the most important basic information about children in Britain today.

This is also the first year in which we have produced *FactFile* Scotland. Again, this seemed an appropriate step, now that devolution means that lead responsibility for children's policy has shifted to the Scottish Parliament and Scottish Executive. This is an exciting development and we hope that *FactFile* Scotland will prove as valuable a tool in Scotland as its counterpart is in Britain. *FactFile* Scotland is available from our Scotland Office, the address of which you will find near the end of this booklet. Since we are now producing *FactFile* Scotland, this *FactFile* no longer contains Scottish statistics, with the exception of a few UK/EU comparisons.

We hope to be able to produce a *FactFile* Wales in due course. Meanwhile, this edition contains some specific information about children in Wales (and England), but most of the data refers to the UK or to Great Britain; some of it refers only to England.

Population

Table 1.1: Population of the United Kingdom (thousands).

	1961	1971	1981	1991	1998	2021
England	43,561	46,412	46,821	48,208	49,495	53,715
Wales	2,635	2,740	2,813	2,891	2,933	3,047
Scotland	5,184	5,236	5,180	5,107	5,120	5,058
Northern Ireland	1,427	1,540	1,538	1,601	1,689	1,821
United Kingdom	52,807	55,928	56,352	57,808	59,237	63,642

Source: *Social Trends 30*, ONS, The Stationery Office, 2000; *FactFile* 2000.

The UK has the 18th largest population in the world. In common with the rest of the EU, the United Kingdom's population is ageing. By 2016 it is expected that, for the first time, the number of people aged 65 and over will exceed those aged under 16.

About 1 person in 15 in Britain is from an ethnic minority group. In general, ethnic minority groups in Britain have a younger age structure than the White population, reflecting past immigration and fertility patterns. The Bangladeshi group has the youngest age structure: 43% of Bangladeshis were under 16 in 1998–99, compared with 20% of White people.

Source: *Social Trends 30*, ONS, The Stationery Office, 2000.

Table 1.2: Population by age and ethnic group, Great Britain, 1998–99[1].

Age group	Under 16	16–34	35–64	65 and over	All ages (= 100%) (millions)
Black-Caribbean	23	29	38	9	0.5
Black-African	32	37	29	2	0.4
Other Black group	43	37	18	–	0.1
All Black groups	29	33	33	6	0.9
Indian	24	32	38	7	0.9
Pakistani	35	36	25	3	0.6
Bangladeshi	43	32	22	3	0.2
All Pakistani/ Bangladeshi	37	35	24	3	1.0
Chinese	15	40	39	6	0.2
None of the above	43	30	24	2	0.8
All other groups[2]	38	32	27	3	1.0
White	20	26	38	16	53.1
All ethnic groups[3]	**21**	**26**	**38**	**15**	**56.8**

1 Population living in private households
2 Includes those of mixed origin.
3 Includes those who did not state their ethnic group.

Source: Labour Force Survey, ONS, reproduced in *Social Trends 30*, The Stationery Office, 2000.

Table 1.3: Numbers of children and young people (mid-1998 resident population).

Numbers of children aged under 16 (thousands)	
Great Britain	11,696.2
England	10,082.9
Wales	599.1
Scotland	1,014.2

In 1998 there were 12,110 (thousands) children aged under 16 in the UK; 6,210 (thousands) boys and 5,900 (thousands) girls.

Source: ONS dataset 2000.

Numbers of live births

In the ten years between 1968 and 1977 in the UK the total number of live births dropped by nearly a third, from 947,000 to 657,000. Between 1978 and 1990, with some fluctuation, there was an increase to 799,000. Since then there has been a steady decrease with the number of live births in 1998 being 717,000, a 10% fall since 1990.

Source: *Social Inequalities,* ONS, The Stationery Office, 2000.

Fertility rates

Changes in fertility patterns influence the size of households and families and also affect the age structure of the population. At the beginning of the 20th century there were about 115 live births per 1,000 women aged 15–44 in the UK, but in 1998 there were less than 60 births per 1,000 women of childbearing age. In the 1970s fertility fell below the level needed for natural population change to keep the population at a stable size, and has remained below that level ever since. In general, fertility rates for older women have increased since the early 1980s while those for younger women have declined. Women aged 25–29 are still the most likely to give birth, but since 1992 those in the 30–34 age group have been more likely to give birth than those aged 20–24.

Source: *Social Trends* 30, ONS, The Stationery Office, 2000.

Births outside marriage

Almost 4 in 10 live births in Great Britain in 1998 occurred outside marriage, more than four times the proportion in 1974. Most of the increase in the number of births outside marriage since the late 1980s has been to cohabiting couples, ie parents living at the same address. In 1998 about four-fifths of births outside marriage were jointly registered by both parents; three-quarters of these births were to parents living at the same address.

Source: *Social Trends* 30, ONS, The Stationery Office, 2000.

Teenage parenthood

The total number of live births to teenage girls in England and Wales peaked at almost 87,000 in 1966.

By 1997 the number of births to teenagers had fallen to 46,000, representing a fall of 47% from their peak compared to a decline of only 24% in the total number of live births over the same period. Despite this fall, in 1995 the UK had the highest rate of live births to teenage women in the EU – over twice the EU average. Births to teenage mothers are particularly likely to take place outside marriage. In 1998 almost 9 in 10 live births to women aged under 20 in England and Wales occurred outside marriage. Mothers in this age group are also the most likely to have a birth outside marriage registered without the father's details: 29% of births to teenage mothers were registered solely by the mother.

Source: *Social Trends 30*, ONS, The Stationery Office, 2000.

The risk of teenage parenthood is greatest for young people who have grown up in poverty and disadvantage or with poor educational achievement. Furthermore, teenage parents tend to remain poor and they are disproportionately likely to suffer relationship breakdown. Their health and that of their children is worse than average.

Source: *Teenage Pregnancy*, Social Exclusion Unit, The Stationery Office, 1999.

Children in families

Table 1.4: Percentage of children living in different family types, Great Britain.

	1972	1981	1991–92	1998–99
Couple families				
1 child	16	18	17	15
2 children	35	41	37	36
3 or more children	41	29	28	26
Lone mother families				
1 child	2	3	5	6
2 children	2	4	7	8
3 or more children	2	3	6	7
Lone father families				
1 child	–	1	–	1
2 or more children	1	1	1	1
All dependent children	100	100	100	100

Source: General Household Survey, ONS, reported in *Social Trends 30*, The Stationery Office, 2000.

Since the 1970s there has been a growth in the proportion of children living in lone parent families, but most children still live in couple families.

Ethnicity and family structure

In spring 1999, 29% of White households in Britain were single person households, compared with 30% of Black households but only 7% of Pakistani/ Bangladeshi households. Households headed by a Pakistani/Bangladeshi, on the other hand, were most likely to contain dependent children. This is partly explained by the young age structure of the South Asian groups. South Asian families also tend to be larger and are more likely to live in households of two or more families, in comparison with other ethnic groups.

In contrast, a relatively high proportion of households headed by a Black person are lone parent families: 24%, compared with 6% of households headed by a White person and 8% of those headed by a Pakistani/Bangladeshi.

Source: *Social Trends 30*, ONS, The Stationery Office, 2000.

Marriage

Marriage is still the usual form of partnership between men and women in the UK. However, the total number of marriages in the UK has fallen from a peak in 1972. In 1997 there were 310,000 marriages, among the lowest figures recorded during the 20th century. In 1997 there were 181,000 first marriages for both partners, less than half the number in 1970. Slightly over two-fifths of marriages in 1997 were remarriages for either or both partners. Following falls in the average age at first marriage between 1919 and 1970, there has been a tendency for people to marry for the first time slightly later in life. Between 1971 and 1997 the mean age at first marriage in England and Wales rose from 24 years to 29 years for men, and from 22 years to 27 years for women.

Source: *Social Trends 30*, ONS, The Stationery Office, 2000.

Children and divorce

There were 1% fewer divorces in England and Wales in 1998 than there were in 1997, the second successive year in which the number of divorces has fallen. The number of divorces in England and Wales involving couples with children under 16 peaked in 1993 at 95,000. In 1998 just over 150,000 children experienced divorce, compared with 176,000 in the peak year, 1993, and only 82,000 in 1971.

In 1998 about 1 in 4 children affected by divorce were under 5 years old and about 7 in 10 were aged under ten years. Almost 1 in 4 children born in 1979 was likely to have been affected by divorce before reaching the age of 16.

Source: *Social Trends 30*, ONS, The Stationery Office, 2000.

Stepfamilies

Stepfamilies can be either married or cohabiting couples. In 1996–97 stepfamilies with dependent children accounted for about 8% of all families with dependent children in Britain where the head of the family was aged under 60. In 84% of stepfamilies at least one child was from a previous relationship of the woman, while in 12% of families there was at least one child from the man's previous relationship. In 4% of stepfamilies there were children from both partners' previous relationships.

Source: *Social Trends 30*, ONS, The Stationery Office, 2000.

Lone parenthood

A noticeable trend in the last couple of decades has been the increase in lone mother families. Before the 1980s much of the increase was due to divorce, while since then single lone motherhood (never married, non-cohabiting women with children) grew at a faster rate.

Table 1.5: Families headed by lone parents as a percentage[1] of all families with dependent children: by marital status.

Great Britain			Percentages		
	1971	1981	1991–92	1996–97	1998–99
Lone mother					
Single	1	2	6	7	9
Widowed	2	2	1	1	1
Divorced	2	4	6	6	8
Separated	2	2	4	5	5
All lone mothers	7	11	18	20	22
Lone father	1	2	1	2	2
Married/ cohabiting couple[2]	92	87	81	79	75
All families with dependent children	**100**	**100**	**100**	**100**	**100**

1 Dependent children are under 16, or 16 to 18 and in full-time education, in the family unit, and living in the household.

2 Includes married women whose husbands are not defined as resident in the household.

Source: General Household Survey, ONS, reported in *Social Trends 30*, The Stationery Office, 2000.

Social exclusion and poverty

Definitions and measures

Poverty is usually taken to refer to a lack of material resources, in particular income. Social exclusion, on the other hand, generally connotes an inability to participate effectively in economic, social, political and cultural life, so that people affected are unable to enjoy the activities or take advantage of opportunities that others take for granted.

There are two approaches to attempting to measure poverty; one sees poverty in absolute terms and tends to emphasise basic physical needs and discounts social and cultural norms. The other views poverty relatively, in terms of generally accepted standards of living in a particular society. There is no official measure of poverty. However, the one which is most frequently used, if not universally accepted, in the UK and across the EU, is '50% of average income'. In Britain this is currently about £10,000 per annum for a family with two children. People whose incomes are below this line are then defined as (relatively) poor. Some critics say this is a measure of inequality rather than of poverty.

The Government has announced its intention to end child poverty by 2020. Alongside this long-term target, it has set out a number of indicators by which it intends to measure its success in tackling poverty and social exclusion as they affect children. They include health and education outcomes which relate to social exclusion, as well as measures of poverty such as 'a reduction in the proportion of children in households with persistently low incomes.' The Government has decided to take '60% of average income' as its 'poverty line'. The Government's progress is also being independently monitored by the New Policy Institute.

Sources: *Opportunity for all: tackling poverty and social exclusion, the first annual report,* DSS, Stationery Office, 1999; *Monitoring poverty and social exclusion* by Catherine Howarth, Peter Kenway, Guy Palmer and Romina Miorellie for the Joseph Rowntree Foundation, New Policy Institute, 1999.

Numbers of children living in poverty

Dependent children's income is largely determined by the financial position of the adults in their households. In 1997–98 about 3.2 million children in Britain were living on incomes of less than 60% of average income. Children are over-represented in the lower end of the income distribution: dependent children make up only about 20% of the British population but account for about 30% of those in the bottom section of the income distribution.

Source: DSS, Households Below Average Income 1994/5–1997/8, reported in *Social Inequalities 2000,* ONS, The Stationery Office, 2000.

Child poverty trends

The proportion of children living in households with relatively low incomes has increased dramatically: in 1995–96, 1 in 3 children lived in households with below half average income, compared with 1 in 10 in 1979.

Source: *Opportunity for all: tackling poverty and social exclusion, the first annual report*, DSS, The Stationery Office, 1999.

An independent study confirms that the Government's anti-poverty measures will lift 1.2 million children out of poverty by April 2002. This should cut the child poverty rate in Britain by about a third, from 26.3% to 17%.

Not all the poor will benefit however. Cuts in lone parent benefit and other changes mean that 1 in 6 children in the poorest tenth of the population will see their household incomes fall.

Note: this study was carried out before the announcement of the outcome of the Government's Spending Review in July 2000 and so does not take into account the impact of any of its programmes.

Source: *How effective is the British Government's attempt to reduce child poverty?* By D. Piachaud and H. Sutherland, Innocenti Working Paper 77, Unicef, 2000.

Children at special risk of poverty

Certain groups of children are particularly likely to be living in households with low incomes. Those most at risk of being in the bottom 30% of the income distribution include children living:

- In larger families (with four or more children). 73% of these are in the bottom 30% of the income distribution.
- In families with young mothers (aged 16–24). 68% are in the bottom 30% of the income distribution.
- In minority ethnic families. 65% are in the bottom 30% of the income distribution.
- In lone parent families where the parent has never been married – a 79% chance; or is divorced or separated, a 66% chance.
- Without a working parent. 86% of these families are in the bottom 30% of the income distribution.
- With parent(s) without educational qualifications – a 54% chance.

Source: Analysis based on the Households Below Average Income data, Analytical Services Division, DSS, reported in *Opportunity for all: tackling poverty and social exclusion, the first annual report*, DSS, The Stationery Office, 1999.

People's incomes fluctuate so many of those classified as poor last year will not be poor this year. The longer a child is poor, the greater the deprivation entailed and the deeper the long-term impact. Research now shows that young children – those of pre-school age – have a disproportionately high risk of experiencing persistent and chronic poverty.

Source: *Poverty among British children: chronic or transitory?* by Jenkins S. and Hill M., Institute for social and economic research at the University of Essex, 2000.

Child poverty and education

Children from disadvantaged homes face greater barriers to achieving their potential at school. There is considerable evidence to show that growing up in a family experiencing financial difficulties damages children's educational performance.

Children going to school in poorer areas (where more than 35% of pupils are in receipt of free school meals) tend to do less well at school – only 41% achieved level 4 or above at Key Stage 2 (age 11) maths test, compared with 59% of all children in 1998. In secondary schools serving 'hard to let' estates, truancy is four times the national average.

Sources: *Persistent poverty and lifetime inequality: the evidence*, CASE LSE, and HM Treasury, 1999; *National curriculum assessments in England*, DfEE, The Stationery Office, 1999; *Bringing Britain back together: a national strategy for neighbourhood renewal*, Social Exclusion Unit, The Stationery Office, 1999. All reported in *Opportunity for all: tackling poverty and social exclusion, the first annual report*, DSS, The Stationery Office, 1999.

Child poverty and health inequalities

Infants and children in social classes IV and V have higher rates of infant mortality and chronic illness than those in social classes I and II. In 1993–95 the infant mortality rate for social class V was 70% higher than the rate for social class I. Children aged up to 15 from unskilled families are five times more likely to die from accidental injury than those from professional families. Children in low-income families are less likely to eat a healthy and balanced diet and are more likely to become smokers. While fruit and vegetable consumption across all income groups is less than the recommended five portions a day, there is a marked trend towards the lowest consumption being among the lower socio-economic groups.

Sources: *Health Inequalities* by Drever F. and Whitehead M. (eds), ONS, The Stationery Office, 1997; *Saving Lives: Our Healthier Nation*, 1999, Department of Health, The Stationery Office; reported in *Opportunity for all: tackling poverty and social exclusion, the first annual report*, DSS, The Stationery Office, 1999.

Child poverty and poor environment

Over 1 in 4 unemployed lone parents with infants live in poor housing, compared with 14% of the population as a whole. Damp, inadequate heating and overcrowding are associated with general ill health and respiratory disorders, accidental injury and emotional problems. Adverse effects on children's health are considered to last into adult life. Fire risk is greatest for those in the poorest social rented housing and temporary accommodation. Children up to the age of 15 from unskilled families are 15 times more likely to die in a fire in the home than those from professional families.

Sources: *English House Condition Survey 1996*, DETR, The Stationery Office 1998; *The health of adult Britain 1841–1994*, by Charlton J. and Murray M. (eds), ONS, 1997; *Does the decline in child mortality vary by social class?* by Roberts and Power, *British Medical Journal*, vol. 313 1996; *Saving Lives: Our Healthier Nation*, Department of Health, The Stationery Office, 1999. All reported in *Opportunity for all: tackling poverty and social exclusion, the first annual report*, DSS, The Stationery Office, 1999.

The geographical distribution of poverty

Table 2.1: Percentage of the regional population living in poverty wards[1] in England and Wales.

Region	%
Merseyside	26
North East	18
North West	8
Yorks and Humberside	6
West Midlands	5
Wales	5
London	4
Eastern	0.1

1 Poverty wards are defined as those within which both the 5% of wards with the highest proportion of people of working age are not working, studying or training and the 5% with the highest concentration of deprived households.

Source: *Poor Areas and Social Exclusion*, CASE paper 35, London: Centre for the Analysis of Social Exclusion, LSE; reported in *Family Poverty and Social Exclusion*, Family Briefing Paper no. 15, Family Policy Studies Centre, 2000.

Poverty is unevenly distributed. In England and Wales, for example, the highest concentration is found in Merseyside where just over a quarter of the population is living in poverty.

Worklessness and child poverty

Nearly 1 in 5 children live in a household where no one works. These families make up the majority of those on low incomes. Not only does this lead to financial disadvantage but as a result, a large proportion of children (2.7 million) are growing up in a household that depends on Income Support or income-based Jobseeker's Allowance as a source of income. Over half of their parents have been on Income Support or income-based Jobseeker's Allowance for more than two years, and 1 in 3 has been claiming for five years or more.

Source: *Labour Force Survey*, ONS, 1999; *Analysis of the cross benefit database*, Analytical Services Division, DSS. Both reported in *Opportunity for all: tackling poverty and social exclusion, the first annual report*, DSS, The Stationery Office, 1999.

Ethnicity, worklessness and poverty

Table 2.2: People in households below 60% median income: by economic status and ethnic group, 1996–98[1].

Great Britain	Percentages					
	White	Black	Indian	Pakistani/ Bangladeshi	Other	All
All above pensionable age	24					24
Other households:						
No members in work	47	52	55	75	40	49
At least one member in work	9		20	56	23	10
All households	17	28	27	64	29	18

1 Combined financial years 1996–97 and 1997–98.

Source: Family Resources Survey, DSS. Reported in *Social Trends 30*, ONS, The Stationery Office, 2000.

Nearly two-thirds of Pakistani and Bangladeshi people live in low income households, compared with over a quarter of Black, Indian and people from other minority ethnic groups and only 17% of White people. The contrasts are even more marked among low income households where at least one member was working. Only 10% of working households on average have low household incomes, but 56% of Pakistani/Bangladeshi working households fall into this category. Indeed, the likelihood of low income among Pakistani/Bangladeshi working households is greater than the likelihood among non-working White households.

Children living in poverty: international comparisons

Table 2.3: Child poverty – the industrialised countries compared.

Child poverty rates		50% of overall median		US official poverty line	
Country	Year	Rate	Rank	Rate	Rank
Russia	1995	26.6	1	98.0	1
US	1994	26.3	2	18.5	12
UK	**1995**	**21.3**	**3**	**28.6**	**10**
Italy	1995	21.2	4	38.1	9
Australia	1994	17.1	5	20.7	11
Canada	1994	16.0	6	9.0	16
Ireland	1987	14.8	7	54.4	6
Poland	1992	14.2	9	90.9	3
Spain	1990	13.1	10	47.3	7
Germany	1994	11.6	11	12.4	14
Hungary	1994	11.5	12	90.6	4
France	1989	9.8	13	17.3	13
Netherlands	1991	8.4	14	10.0	15
Switzerland	1982	6.3	15	1.6	24
Taiwan	1995	6.3	16	4.3	20
Luxembourg	1994	6.3	17	1.1	25
Belgium	1992	6.1	18	7.9	17
Denmark	1992	5.9	19	4.6	19
Austria	1987	5.6	20	5.4	18
Norway	1995	4.5	21	2.8	22
Sweden	1992	3.7	22	3.7	21
Finland	1991	3.4	22	2.6	23
Slovakia	1992	2.2	24	95.2	2
Czech Republic	1992	1.8	25	85.1	5

Source: *Child poverty across industrialised nations,* by Bradbury B. and Jantii M., 1999, Innocenti working paper no. 71, Unicef. Reported in *Family Poverty and Social Exclusion,* Family Briefing Paper no. 15, Family Policy Studies Centre, 2000.

Child poverty rates in the world's wealthiest nations vary from under 3% to over 25%. One in every six of the rich world's children is living in poverty. In total, approximately 47 million children in the nations of the OECD live below their national poverty line. The countries with the lowest child poverty rates allocate the highest proportions of GNP to social expenditure. The measure used by international studies of poverty classifies children as being in poverty if they live in households with less than half the national median (average) income before housing costs. Using this relative measure, the UK has the third worst rate of child poverty across the industrialised world. Only Russia and the US, where 1 in 4 children live in poverty, have a higher rate of child poverty than the UK. If the less generous US poverty line is used (a more 'absolute' poverty measure), the UK's world ranking would fall to tenth and the two countries with the apparent best record on child poverty, Slovakia and the Czech Republic, would rise to 2nd and 5th respectively.

Source: *Child poverty across industrialised nations,* by Bradbury B. and Jantii M., 1999, Innocenti working paper no. 71, Unicef. Reported in *Family Poverty and Social Exclusion,* Family Briefing Paper no. 15, Family Policy Studies Centre, 2000.

The longer-term impact of poverty on children's futures

Key findings include the following:

- Poverty in childhood increases the likelihood of low income in adulthood;
- There is a strong association between children's earnings and those of their parents. Only a third of boys whose fathers were in the bottom quarter of the income distribution made it to the top half when they grew up and the pattern is similar for girls. Men whose fathers were unemployed were twice as likely to be unemployed for a year or more between the ages of 23 and 33;
- People's chances of being in a manual occupation, having no access to a car and living in rented accommodation are also higher if their parents were in the same position.

Sources: *Intergenerational and life course transmission of social exclusion,* by Hobcraft J., Centre for the Analysis of Social Exclusion, paper 15, LSE, 1998; *Childhood disadvantage and intergenerational transmission of economic status,* in *Persistent poverty and lifetime inequality: the evidence,* Centre for the Analysis of Social Exclusion, LSE, and HM Treasury; *Intergenerational mobility among the rich and poor: results from the National Child Development Study,* by Johnson P. and Reed H., Oxford Review of Economic Policy 1996. All reported in *Opportunity for all: tackling poverty and social exclusion, the first annual report,* DSS, The Stationery Office, 1999.

The impact of poverty on children's aspirations

Children in low income families tend to have lower aspirations and expectations for their future. They are much more likely to want jobs that typically take a minimal amount of time to train for and, on the whole, require few, if any, academic qualifications.

Source: *Small expectations: learning to be poor?* Shropshire J. and Middleton S., Joseph Rowntree Foundation, 1999.

Young people's participation in education and the labour market

The number of young people aged 16 to 24 either in work or available for work in the UK fell by nearly a million between 1971 and 1997. One of the reasons is because there are fewer young people than 30 years ago, since the birth rate was low in the second half of the 1970s.

In addition, a much higher proportion of those of compulsory school-leaving age continue in full time education than previously, probably in recognition of the higher level of skills and qualifications now required by employers.

Source: Information from the Census and *Labour Force survey*, ONS, reported in *Social Trends 30*, The Stationery Office, 2000.

Youth unemployment

Table 2.4: Unemployment[1] rates by gender and age.

United Kingdom		Percentages		
	1991	1997	1998	1999
Males				
16–17	15.4	19.3	18.0	21.6
18–24	15.7	14.8	13.0	12.5
25–44	8.0	7.0	5.8	5.6
45–54	6.3	6.1	4.8	4.9
55–59	8.4	8.0	6.7	6.4
60–64	9.9	7.6	7.0	6.4
65 and over	5.9	4.0	–	–
All aged 16 and over	9.2	8.1	6.8	6.8
Females				
16–17	14.3	16.0	15.2	14.0
18–24	10.5	9.7	9.3	9.3
25–44	7.1	5.4	5.2	4.8
45–54	4.6	3.8	3.1	3.2
55–59	5.5	4.8	3.5	3.6
60 and over	4.4	2.0	2.0	1.9
All aged 16 and over	7.2	5.8	5.3	5.1

1 At spring each year. Unemployment based on the ILO definition as a percentage of all economically active.

Source: Labour Force Survey, ONS, produced in *Social Trends 30*, ONS, The Stationery Office, 2000.

Young people are much more likely to be unemployed than older people. In spring 1999, 21.6% of 16 and 17-year-old men, and 14% of women of the same age, were unemployed. The rates for 18 to 24-year-olds were lower at 12.5% and 9.3% respectively, but these were still almost double the rates for all people of working age.

The New Deal for young people

In April 1998 the Government introduced the New Deal for young unemployed people as part of its Welfare to Work strategy. The aim of the programme is to help young people who have been unemployed and claiming Job Seekers' Allowance for six months or more, to find work and to improve their long-term employability. At the end of February 2000 there were about 130,000 young people on the New Deal in Britain, three-quarters of them male.

Research has found that the New Deal has made a real difference to young people. Of the young people who had been through the programme, just under half had so far found work. An encouraging proportion of the jobs were sustained: 3 in 4 of the young people who found jobs were still in them three months later. Some of them would probably have got jobs anyway, perhaps half of these young people. Nevertheless, the New Deal is estimated to have led to a reduction in youth unemployment by about 30,000 in its first year.

Source: *Keeping track of welfare reform: the New Deal programme,* by Millar J., Joseph Rowntree Foundation, 2000.

It has, however, been alleged that young people on the New Deal are getting a raw deal from employers who use them as cheap labour and offer them little if any training. In a survey 44% of participating firms – which receive £60 per week for six months for every person they take on – said the subsidy payment was the main reason for signing up to the New Deal.

Source: *What works? Young people and employers on the New Deal,* The Prince's Trust, 2000.

Government research also suggests that young people from minority ethnic communities are less likely than their White counterparts to move from the New Deal to permanent jobs, despite having better qualifications. However, once in work they were found to be less likely to drop out than White young people. Part of the gap may be due to the fact that many Black and Asian young people live in inner city areas where the chance of finding work is lower for everyone. Racism in the labour market is another probable cause.

Source: Information from *Labour Market Trends*, ONS 2000 discussed in "*New Deal less likely to benefit ethnic minority youths*", *The Guardian*, 11/2/2000.

Education and training

Government spending on education

Total Government expenditure on education in the UK in 1997–98 was about £39.1 billion, 4.8% of GDP, down from 5.1% of GDP in 1995–96 and 5% in 1996–97.

Source: DfEE, National Assembly for Wales, Scottish Executive, Dept. of Education Northern Ireland, reproduced in *Social Trends 30*, ONS, The Stationery Office, 2000.

Schools and pupils

In 1998–99 in the UK there were over 10 million full-time and part-time pupils in 33.5 thousand schools.

Table 3.1: School pupils[1] by type of school, United Kingdom.

	Thousands				
	1970/71	1980/81	1990/91	1994/95	1998/99[2]
Public sector schools[3]					
Nursery[4]	50	89	105	111	109
Primary	5,902	5,171	4,955	5,230	5,376
Secondary Modern	1,164	233	94	90	92
Grammar	673	149	156	184	203
Comprehensive[5]	1,313	3,730	2,843	3,093	3,205
Other secondary	403	434	300	289	291
All public sector schools	9,507	9,806	843	8,996	9,276
Non-maintained schools[3]	621	619	613	600	616

Continued overleaf.

Table 3.1: continued

	Thousands				
	1970/71	1980/81	1990/91	1994/95	1998/99[2]
Special schools[6]	103	148	114	117	115
Pupil referral units					9
All schools	10,230	10,572	9,180	9,714	10,016

1 Head counts.
2 All data for Wales and for nursery schools in Scotland are for 1997–98.
3 Excludes special schools.
4 Nursery classes within primary schools are included in primary schools except for Scotland in 1990/91 when they are included in nursery schools.
5 Excludes sixth form colleges from 1980/81.
6 Includes maintained and non-maintained sectors.

Source: DfEE, National Assembly for Wales, Scottish Executive, Dept. of Education Northern Ireland, reproduced in *Social Trends 30*, ONS, The Stationery Office, 2000.

The early years

Special help for vulnerable young children

In April 1999 the Government launched the Sure Start programme in 21 neighbourhoods, a package relating to childcare, health, education and the family which aims to assist children in their early years, particularly those from disadvantaged backgrounds. The Government announced a further expansion of Sure Start in its Spending Review in July 2000.

Day care

Table 3.2: Day care places for children[1], England and Wales.

	Thousands			
	1987	1992	1997	1998
Day nurseries				
Local authority provided	29	24	20	19
Registered	32	96	180	211
Non-registered[2]	1	1	2	1
After school clubs				97
All day nursery places	62	122	202	329
Childminders				
Local authority provided	2	2	4	4
Other registered person	152	262	379	384
All childminder places	153	265	383	388
Playgroups				
Local authority provided	3	2	2	1
Registered	423	434	408	407
Non-registered	7	3	3	1
All playgroup places	433	439	413	410

1 Under the age of eight.
2 England only.

Source: DfEE, National Assembly for Wales, reported in *Social Trends 30*, ONS, The Stationery Office, 2000.

Day care facilities are provided for young children by childminders, voluntary agencies, private nurseries and local authorities, as well as nannies and relatives. In 1998 there were about 1.1 million places with childminders, in playgroups and day nurseries for children under eight in England and Wales. The numbers of places in day nurseries and with childminders have shown particularly large increases since the late 1980s, whereas those in playgroups have declined. In 1987 there were around 60,000 places in day nurseries in England and Wales compared with over 300,000 in 1998. After school clubs (held before or after school) have been introduced in recent years and in 1998 there were 97,000 such places in England and Wales. Historically, the provision of day care in the UK has lagged behind that in other European countries: under the Government's National Childcare Strategy the gap is steadily being closed.

Early years education

The expansion of education for children aged under five is one of the most striking trends in education in the UK. The Government is committed to the provision of a free school place for every four-year-old in England whose parents want it and also to extending the provision for three-year-olds. (A 'place' is defined as a two-and-a-half hour session up to five times a week, 33 weeks a year). In 1970–71 about 20% of three and four-year-olds in the UK attended school but by 1998–99 this had risen to 62%. Attendance at nursery schools and primary schools in England varies widely between the Government Office Regions: the percentage ranged from 84% in the North East to under 50% in the East of England, the South East and the South West.

In January 1999, 98% of all four-year-olds in England were in early years provision: 78% were in maintained nursery and primary schools, 15% in the private and voluntary sector and 5% in independent schools.

Source: DfEE, National Assembly for Wales, Scottish Executive, Dept. of Education Northern Ireland, reproduced in *Social Trends 30*, ONS, The Stationery Office, 2000.

Over the last year there has been some criticism of the Government's policy of encouraging children to enter nursery classes in primary school, on the grounds that beginning 'formal' education at so young an age may be detrimental to children's educational and social development. Critics point to academic research suggesting that late maturing boys, in particular, may benefit from a later start to formal instruction. Certainly, Britain is out of step with most other European countries in its statutory age of school entry. Six years is the usual age of entry, except in Scandinavia where it is seven.

Source: *The International Educational Achievement study of reading literacy: achievement and instruction in 32 school systems*, by Elley W.B. (ed), International Studies in Educational Achievement, Oxford, Pergamon Elsevier 1992; cited in *Starting school: do our children start too young?* by Wolff S., in *Young Minds* magazine, edition 42, 1999.

Class sizes and pupil/teacher ratios

The average class size in primary schools in the UK in 1998–99 was 27.1 pupils. The average class size in secondary schools in Great Britain was 21.7 pupils. Between 1995–96 and 1998–99 the percentage of classes with more than 30 pupils fell in all the regions of England, with the exception of the East of England where it remained at 18%. In contrast, the percentage in Scotland increased from 13% in 1995–96 to 16% over the three years, although the average class sizes in Scotland (at its equivalent of Key Stage 1) continued to be smaller than those in most of the regions of England. Wales has the lowest average class size at Key Stage 1 and the lowest proportion of classes with more than 30 pupils.

The average pupil/teacher ratio in nursery schools in 1998–99 was 20.6. In primary schools the pupil/teacher ratio was 23.0 and in secondary schools it was 16.5. The average teacher/pupil ratio for all schools was 18.2 compared to 17.3 in 1990–91.

Sources: *Education and Training Statistics for the UK*, DfEE, National Assembly for Wales, Scottish Executive, Dept. of Education Northern Ireland, The Stationery Office, 1999; *Social Trends 30*, ONS, The Stationery Office, 2000.

Educational attainment: trends and variations by region, gender and ethnicity

In recent years the proportion of pupils in the UK achieving GCSEs has increased significantly. In England for example, in 1974–75 just over a fifth of students gained five O levels/CSEs at grades A to C. By 1997–98 the proportion achieving similar grades in GCSEs had risen to almost half. While most young people achieve graded results, a small minority do not: in 1974–75 the proportion was 20% but by 1997–98 this had fallen to just over 6%. Higher proportions of girls achieve good GCSE results compared with boys: in 1997–98 c.40% of boys achieved five or more GCSEs at grades A to C compared to over 50% of girls.

Source: *Statistics of Education, Public Examinations GCSE/GNVQ and GCE/GNVQ in England for 1998*, DfEE, 1999, The Stationery Office, reproduced in *Social Inequalities*, ONS, The Stationery Office, 2000.

Table 3.3: Examination achievements of pupils in schools by region and gender, 1997–98.

	Percentages					
	2 or more GCE A levels[1]		5 or more GCSEs grades A–C[2]		No graded GCSEs[2]	
	M	F	M	F	M	F
Great Britain	26	33	42	52	8	5
North East	19	25	35	43	10	7
North West	25	31	39	49	9	6
Yorkshire and the Humber	22	27	36	46	10	7
East Midlands	26	32	40	51	7	5
West Midlands	25	31	38	48	8	6
Eastern	31	36	46	56	6	4
London	26	33	40	51	8	5
South East	32	39	47	58	7	5
South West	28	37	46	57	6	4
England	27	33	41	52	8	5
Wales	23	30	40	51	11	8
Scotland	25	33	50	61	5	4

1 Pupils aged 17 to 19 at the end of the school year in England and Wales as a percentage of the 18-year-old population. For Scotland the figures relate to pupils in years S5/S6 gaining three or more SCE Higher passes as a percentage of the 17-year-old population.

2 Pupils aged 16 at the end of the school year as a percentage of the 15-year-old population at start of school year. Scotland pupils are in year S4.

Source: *Social Trends 30*, ONS, The Stationery Office, 2000.

There are regional variations in educational attainment. Overall, the highest achievement levels for boys and girls in 1997–98 were in Scotland. Within England, girls outperformed boys in all regions, with the South of the country showing generally higher levels of achievements than the North. Although the proportion of pupils achieving five GCSEs A to C was similar in England and Wales, the proportion achieving no graded results was higher in Wales. Eleven per cent of boys in Wales achieved no graded results in 1997–98, compared with 8% in England and 5% in Scotland.

In England and Wales in 1998 over half the pupils of Indian origin and just under a half of all White pupils gained five GCSEs A to C, but less than a third of Black or Pakistani/Bangladeshi did.

Although the proportion achieving good grades has been improving for all ethnic groups, Bangladeshi pupils in particular have been progressing rapidly and significantly.

More than double the proportion of Bangladeshi students gained five GCSEs grades A to C in 1998 than in 1992. In 1998, 33% received five GCSEs at grades A to C compared with only 14% in 1992.

Source: *Youth Cohort Study: The activities and experiences of 16-year-olds in England and Wales 1998*, issue no. 4, 1999, The Stationery Office; reproduced in *Social Inequalities*, ONS, The Stationery Office, 2000.

Post-compulsory education

In recent years the numbers of young people going on to A levels or their equivalent or taking up vocational courses has been increasing. Between 1988 and 1998, the proportion of 16–18-year-olds in education and training in England and Wales rose from 62% to 74%. Most of this increase took place at the start of the 1990s. Since then there has been more stability in the proportions in education and training. In 1998 about half of all 16 to 18-year-olds were in full-time education. The rest participated in part-time courses or Government supported training schemes, entered the labour market, or did none of these things.

Source: *Participation in education and training by 16–18-year-olds in England 1988–98,* DfEE, 1999; reported in *Social Inequalities,* ONS, The Stationery Office, 2000.

16–18-year-olds not in education, employment or training and unemployment

At any one time it is estimated that about 9% of 16–18-year-olds are not in education, employment or training. The young people who are most likely to be in this group are those who have not achieved well in education and/or who have experienced problems with truancy and exclusion.

Being out of education, employment or training for more than six months between the ages 16–18 is the most powerful predictor of unemployment at age 21.

Sources: *Participation in education and training by 16–18-year-olds in England 1988–98,* DfEE, 1999, reported in *Social Inequalities,* ONS, The Stationery Office 2000; *Bridging the gap: new opportunities for 16–18-year-olds not in education, employment or training,* The Stationery Office, 1999.

International comparisons

Although young people in the UK are increasingly likely to continue with their education, compared with the rest of the EU the UK has one of the lowest full-time participation rates of 16, 17 and 18-year-olds in secondary and tertiary education. In 1996 full-time participation rates of 18-year-olds in secondary education varied between 17% in Greece and 93% in Sweden. In the UK the rate was just over 35%.

Source: OECD, 1999, reported in *Social Trends 30*, ONS, The Stationery Office, 2000.

Britain has one of the worst records in the industrialised world for getting young people successfully from school into work. Research carried out in 1998 found that of 14 countries studied in depth, only Hungary and Portugal had a record as poor as the UK for smoothing the transition to work. The study found that in Britain, more than a quarter of young people who stayed on at school after the end of compulsory education dropped out within a year. In only three other countries – Spain, Hungary and Mexico – did 20% or more drop out of education within a year.

In Britain, 10% of young people disappeared between education, training and work and were deemed to be 'at risk'; and 40% of 19 to 24-year-olds failed to achieve what the study considered to be the minimum qualifications necessary for holding down a job.

Source: *Thematic review of the transition from initial education to working life* by the Organisation for Economic Co-operation and Development (OECD), 2000.

Achievement at A level and equivalent

Overall, there has been an increase in the proportion of young men and women in the UK achieving two or more A levels or equivalent. The proportion of young women achieving this has doubled since the mid-1970s to 25%. The increase in the proportion of young men achieving this has been more modest, with a rise of just under a half over the same period.

In 1987–88 an equal proportion of young men and women achieved two or more A levels or equivalent (15%) but since 1988–89 women have outperformed men.

Source: DfEE, National Assembly for Wales, Scottish Executive, Dept. of Education Northern Ireland. Reported in *Social Trends 30*, ONS, The Stationery Office, 2000.

Further and higher education

Accompanying the expansion of pupils staying on after the school leaving age, there has been an increase in the numbers going into further and higher education. Since the start of the 1970s the numbers in further education have fluctuated but there has been an overall increase from around 1.7 million in 1970–71 to over 2.4 million in 1997–98.

In 1970–71 there were about 725,000 women in further education but by 1997–98 this had doubled to about 1.4 million. The rise in the numbers of men in further education was more modest.

Over the same period, the numbers of students in higher education have more than trebled, from 620,000 to almost two million. A large part of this increase is due again to more women entering higher education. In 1970–71 women made up just under a third of the higher education population but by 1997–98 there were more women than men in higher education, about one million women and 900,000 men.

Source: *Social Inequalities,* ONS, The Stationery Office, 2000.

Children with special educational needs

(Also see Table 3.1 on page 29).

There were 289,000 full and part-time pupils with special educational needs (SEN) in the UK in 1998–99, representing 3% of all pupils, with 96% of them being in maintained schools.

Most children with SEN in the UK are educated in mainstream schools: just over a third (35%) are in special schools, 0.7% are in pupil referral units, 28% are in maintained primary schools and 31% are in maintained secondary schools.

Sources: *Education and Training Statistics for the UK 1999,* DfEE, National Assembly for Wales, Scottish Executive, Dept. of Education Northern Ireland, The Stationery Office, 1999; *Social Trends 30*, ONS, The Stationery Office, 2000.

Bullying

A survey carried out in 2000 suggested that a third of pupils in England and Wales had been bullied during the last 12 months. A quarter of the young people taking part in the survey had been threatened at school and 13% had been attacked, of whom there were three times more boys as girls. One in 11 said they had missed school through fear of violence. Pupils in Wales felt under the greatest threat, but the greatest number of attacks took place in the South West of England.

In all, 39% of respondents in Wales said their teachers were unaware of bullying, compared with 25% in the North West, 27% in Yorkshire and Humberside, and 30% in London and the South East. Schools in the North West appear to have been more successful in tackling the problem, with just under two-thirds of respondents from that region saying that they had never been bullied and three-quarters reporting that their teachers were aware of the issue. Bullying appeared to be most widespread in the Midlands, with 43% of respondents saying that they had been victims.

The implication of this survey is that bullying remains a serious problem in many schools, despite the continuing efforts of policy makers and schools to eradicate it.

Source: Representative survey commissioned by the Association of teachers and lecturers from MORI. 2,610 children interviewed. Reported in "Third of all pupils bullied in past year", in the *Times* newspaper, 17/4/2000.

Truancy and school exclusions

Table 3.4: Permanent exclusion rates[1] by ethnic group, England, January 1998.

	Percentages
White	0.17
Black Caribbean	0.76
Black African	0.29
Black Other	0.57
Indian	0.06
Pakistani	0.13
Bangladeshi	0.09
Chinese	0.05
All	0.18

1 Number of permanent exclusions as a percentage of the number of full and part-time pupils of all ages.

Source: DfEE, reproduced in *Social Trends 30*, ONS, The Stationery Office, 2000.

Although truancy and social exclusion are separate issues, the risk factors and outcomes associated with them are often similar. In 1998 the Social Exclusion Unit reported on both issues, and highlighted the lack of reliable truancy figures.

Official figures show relatively low and stable levels of about 1% of school time lost to unauthorised absence in a year, although many surveys show that around a third of pupils truant at least occasionally. Analysis of the Youth Cohort Study suggests that truants' parents are more likely than other parents to be in low skilled jobs or to be out of work.

In 1994–95 about 11,000 pupils were permanently excluded from school in England. The figure rose to over 12,600 in 1996–97. In 1997–98 the number fell slightly to just under 12,300. Overall, permanent exclusions only affect a tiny section of the school population – about 16 per 10,000 pupils were permanently excluded in England in 1997–98.

There are major differences in the distribution of exclusions. Most exclusions occur in secondary schools, particularly to children aged 13 to 15. Boys are much more likely to be excluded than girls: in England in 1997–98, over four-fifths of excluded pupils were boys. Children with special educational needs and those in care are both over-represented within the population of pupils excluded from school. In England in 1997–98 children with statements of special educational need were almost seven times more likely to be permanently excluded than those without. Young Black Caribbeans are also over-represented in the excluded group. In 1997–98 the exclusion rate among this group in England was around four times the exclusion rate for the whole school population.

Non-attendance at school has implications for educational attainment and for outcomes in adulthood. A recent Youth Cohort Study report showed that in 1998 just under a third of persistent truants reported they had no qualifications at year 11, compared with about 4% of non-truants. Persistent truants are four times more likely not to be in education, employment or training at age 16 than other children. There is a strong association between non-attendance at school and crime. The Home Office has found that truants were more than three times as likely to offend than non-truants. Almost half of all school age offenders have been excluded from school.

Sources: *Misspent youth – young people and crime,* Audit Commission, 1996; *Young people and crime – Home Office research study no. 45,* by Graham J. and Bowling B., Home Office, 1995; *Truancy and school exclusion,* Social Exclusion Unit, The Stationery Office, 1999; *Statistical bulletin: pupil absence and truancy from schools in England 1998–9,* issue no. 15/99, DfEE, The Stationery Office; *Youth cohort study: the activities and experiences of 16 and 17-year-olds: England and Wales,* issue no 4, DfEE, The Stationery Office, 1998; *Permanent exclusions from schools in England 1997–98 and exclusion appeals lodged by parents in England 1997–98,* DfEE, 1999; *Truancy and youth transitions: youth cohort study report no. 34,* by Casey B. and Smith D., DfEE, 1995. All reported in *Social Inequalities,* ONS, The Stationery Office, 2000.

Child protection

Children on child protection registers

Children who are considered to be suffering from or likely to suffer significant harm and for whom there is a child protection plan have their names registered on a central child protection register held by each local social services department in the UK. Registration takes place following a child protection case conference, at which professionals make decisions about whether the level of risk to the child is sufficient for the child's name to be placed on the register. If the child is registered, an inter-agency child protection plan is drawn up and agreed between the professionals involved with the child and his or her family.

There are four main categories of child abuse under which a child's name can be registered: neglect, physical abuse, sexual abuse and emotional abuse. Where registration is required or necessary, a child is usually registered under one main category of abuse but may be registered under more.

Numbers on child protection registers in England

Table 4.1: Children and young people on child protection registers in England at 31 March 1999, by age and gender.

	Age at 31 March 1999					
	All ages	Under 1	1–4	5–9	10–15	16 and over
Numbers[1]						
All children[2]	31,900	3,000	9,700	9,700	8,600	600
Boys	16,000	1,500	5,000	5,000	4,200	300
Girls	15,600	1,500	4,700	4,700	4,400	400
Rates[3]						
All children	28	50	39	30	23	5
Boys	28	50	39	30	22	4
Girls	28	50	39	29	24	6

1 Figures may not add due to rounding.
2 The 'All ages, all children' figures include 300 unborn children.
3 Rates are per 10,000 population in each age and gender group.

Source: *Children and Young People on Child Protection Registers – Year ending 31 March 1999, England,* Department of Health, 1999.

- On 31 March 1999 there were a total of 31,900 children on child protection registers in England, 1% more than the previous year. This represents a rate of 28 children per 10,000 in the population aged under 18. The numbers on registers reached 45,000 in 1991 but then fell sharply over the next two years. Since then the numbers have been relatively stable.

- Of the 31,900 children on child protection registers, 16,000 (51%) were boys and 15,600 (49%) were girls.
- At 31 March 1999 there were 3,000 children under one year of age, 9% of the total, a proportion which has risen slowly over the previous decade. At the other end of the age range 600 or 2% were aged 16 and over; this number has been falling steadily.

Registrations to child protection registers in England

Table 4.2: Registrations to and de-registrations from child protection registers by gender, at 31 March 1999, England.

	All children[1]	Boys	Girls
Registrations	30,100	14,700	14,600
De-registrations	29,600	14,900	14,700

1 The 'All children' figures include unborn children.

Source: *Children and Young People on Child Protection Registers – Year ending 31 March 1999 England,* Department of Health, 1999.

These figures correspond to 27 per 10,000 registrations and 26 per 10,000 de-registrations.

Children aged under one had the highest registration rate (71 per 10,000 children in that age group). The rate was lower for the age group one to four (35) and continues to decline up the age range, falling to four for children aged over 15. For numbers on the register the pattern was similar although the differences between age groups were less marked.

Re-registrations to child protection registers in England

Of the 30,100 registrations in the year ending 31 March 1999 it is estimated that 4,600 (15%) were re-registrations, ie children who had been on the register previously. This represents a sharp fall from the figure of 19% a year earlier, after having risen steadily since 1992 when figures were first collected.

In November 1998 the Department of Health established 're-registrations to the child protection register' as an indicator of children's social services under the Quality Protects programme. The Department has also set the related National Priorities Guidance target to: "reduce by 10% by 2002, the proportion of children who are re-registered on the child protection register, from a baseline for the year ending March 1997." This target would require a reduction from the 1996–97 figure of 19.4% to 17.2% by 2001–02.

Source: *Children and Young People on Child Protection Registers – Year ending 31 March 1999, England,* Department of Health, 1999.

Length of time on the register in England

Information was collected about the time that children who were de-registered had spent on the register. During the year ending 31 March 1999, it is estimated that about 7,600 children (25%) had been on the register for under six months, and 4,200 (14%) had been on the register for two years or more. The equivalent percentages a year earlier were 26% and 13% respectively. The percentage of children leaving the register who had been on it for more than two years fell between 1994 and 1996 but has now levelled off. This measure has also been established as an indicator of children's social services under the Quality Protects programme and should be considered alongside the indicator of re-registrations described above.

Categories of abuse: England

Table 4.3: Registrations to child protection registers by category of abuse in England, numbers and percentages.

Category of abuse	Registrations 1998	Registrations 1999	On the register 1998	On the register 1999
Neglect	11,600	12,600	13,000	13,900
Physical injury	9,900	9,400	9,900	9,100
Sexual abuse	6,100	5,800	6,700	6,600
Emotional abuse	4,800	4,800	5,200	5,400
Categories not recommended by 'Working Together'	200	400	300	500
No category available	500	500	200	200
Percentages				
Neglect	39	42	41	44
Physical injury	33	31	31	29
Sexual abuse	20	19	21	21
Emotional abuse	16	16	16	17
Categories not recommended by 'Working Together'	1	1	1	1
No category available	2	2	1	1

Note: The total of the percentages exceed 100 because children in 'mixed' categories are counted more than once.

Source: Information drawn from *Children and Young People on Child Protection Registers – Year Ending 31 March 1999*, England, Department of Health, 1999.

Similar patterns are seen for both registrations and numbers. Neglect is the most commonly used category, being used for 42% of children registered during 1998–99. This proportion has risen steadily since 1995, when 30% of registrations involved neglect. The number of cases for which emotional abuse has been recorded has also risen over the same period. In contrast, the use of the physical injury and emotional abuse categories has steadily fallen.

During 1998–99 girls had a higher rate of registration because of a risk of sexual abuse than boys. For sexual abuse the rate of registration was six per 10,000 girls and four per 10,000 boys in the population. This abuse category accounted for 23% of registrations for girls during the year and 16% of registrations for boys. Boys were more likely to be placed on the register because of a risk of physical injury than girls. For boys, 33% of registrations were in connection with physical injury compared with 30% for girls.

Source: *Children and Young People on Child Protection Registers – Year Ending 31 March 1999*, England, Department of Health, 1999.

Looked after children on the register in England

- At 31 March 1999, 7,900 children (25% of those on the register) in England were looked after by local authorities. This figure represents 15% of all children looked after at that date.
- Sixty-four per cent of these looked after children were subject to care orders with most of the remainder looked after under voluntary agreements. Two-thirds were accommodated in foster placements, a proportion similar to that for

all looked after children, with a further 8% in children's homes and 18% placed with parents.

Source: *Children and Young People on Child Protection Registers – Year Ending 31 March 1999*, England, Department of Health, 1999.

Children and young people on child protection registers in Wales

- On 31 March 1998 there were 2,473 children on child protection registers in Wales, an increase of 448 on the previous year and representing a rate of 37 per 10,000 children aged under 18. The highest rates were in the 1–4 years age group for girls and the under one year age group for boys; for the older age groups the rate decreased as the age increased. The overall rates on the register were higher for girls than boys. Compared to 1992, a lower proportion of children on the registers were in the 5–9 years and 16–17 years age groups.

- There were 2,025 registrations and 2,039 de-registrations. Thirty-one per cent of the registrations were recorded in the neglect (only) category, 26% under physical abuse (only), 11% under sexual abuse (only) and 22% under emotional abuse.

- Physical abuse was involved in 34% of cases registered and sexual abuse was involved in 15% of cases. As in England, neglect (only) was the largest category for both boys and girls. The trend since 1994 has been a fall in the proportion of cases categorised as sexual abuse (only), with considerable increases in those recorded under emotional abuse and neglect.

Source: *Child Protection Register: Statistics for Wales 1998*, Welsh Office, 1999.

The Children Act and the courts

Public law cases are those usually brought by local authorities or the NSPCC and include matters such as care, supervision and emergency protection orders. (Private law cases are brought by private individuals and are generally connected with divorce or parental separation.)

Public law cases must start in the family proceedings court but may be transferred up to the county court to minimise delay, consolidate with other family proceedings, or where the matter is exceptionally grave, complex or important. There are four ways in which the court can deal with an application for an order in public law:

1. An application can be withdrawn but only by order of the court;
2. An application for an order can be refused: in public law proceedings an order is refused if the grounds are not proved and the court has dismissed the application;
3. Make an order of 'no order': this is the outcome if the court has applied the principle of non-intervention under section 1(5) of the Act. This provides that the court shall not make an order unless it considers that doing so would be better for the child than not making an order at all;
4. Make the order which has been applied for.

Table 4.4: Disposal of selected applications in public law in all tiers of court[1], 1998.

Nature of application	Application withdrawn	Orders refused	Orders of no order	Orders made
Care	547	43	121	6,017
Contact with a child in care	214	138	80	1331
Discharge of care	129	44	3	633
Refusal of care-contact	56	37	21	1,104
Emergency protection order	133	42	12	2,612
Secure accommodation	121	8	15	1,142
Supervision	91	4	20	1,006
Supervision order-discharge	18	6	–	52
Section 8(1):				
Residence	118	39	12	890
Contact	126	51	50	731
Prohibited steps	15	3	1	169
Specific issue	12	6	1	74

1 Contains imputed data.

Source: *Judicial Statistics 1998*, The Lord Chancellor's Department, The Stationery Office, 1999.

Child prostitution

It has been estimated that 5,000 minors are involved in prostitution in Britain at any one time.

The key findings of the most recent authoritative research study on this issue are:

Age of involvement in prostitution

- 64% of the sample became involved in prostitution before they could legally consent to sex.
- The youngest children became involved in prostitution aged 11.
- 48% were involved in prostitution before they were 14.
- 72% thought there were now more children on the streets than when they started out.

Abuse and family conflict

- 42% said their first sexual experience was of abuse, and of these, 26% said it occurred before they were ten years old.
- 8% said their first sexual experience took place in the context of prostitution.
- 72% said they experienced conflict or abuse in their family.
- 48% experienced violence at the hands of partners, pimps or punters.

Looked after children

- Almost two-thirds of those questioned aged 18 or under had been in care compared to a third of over 25s.
- This younger group of 'looked after' children – those 25 or younger had also become involved in prostitution at the youngest age, with over half becoming involved before the age of 14.
- Three-quarters of those who ran away from care became involved in prostitution before they were 14.

Runaways

- Almost two-thirds (60%) of all those surveyed had run away and a third had become involved in prostitution while on the run from home or care.
- More than a third had become caught up in prostitution to survive while on the run.

Drug use

- Fifty-six per cent were using drugs such as heroin, crack, and/or amphetamines.
- Drug use was far higher in the younger age group (25 and under); three-quarters of those using drugs before becoming involved in prostitution were in the younger age group.
- Sixty-five per cent of the sample using drugs started after becoming involved in prostitution.

Source: *One Way Street? Retrospectives on Childhood Prostitution*, by Melrose M., Barrett D. and Brodie I., The Children's Society, 1999.

Children and domestic violence

- Ninety per cent of incidents of domestic violence occur when a child is in the same room or next door. Three out of every five children in every classroom are estimated to have witnessed domestic violence of some kind.

Source: *British Crime Survey 1992* quoted in *A Review of Children's Service Development (1995–98) at Refuge*, written for The King's Fund, Refuge, 1998.

NCH published the first study carried out in Britain on the impact of domestic violence on children. 108 women, who had 246 children living with them, completed questionnaires. Further in-depth interviews were carried out with mothers and children. The research found:

- Nearly three-quarters (73%) of mothers said their children had witnessed violent incidents, and 67% had seen their mothers being beaten. Ten per cent of the women had been sexually abused in front of their children.
- Most (91%) of the mothers believed their children were affected in the short-term. A quarter said their children had become aggressive towards them and other children and almost a third had developed problems at school.
- Over 70% said their children had been frightened, 48% that they had become withdrawn and 34% said they had developed bed-wetting problems.
- Around 86% of mothers believed their children were affected in the long term. Thirty-three per

cent thought they had become violent, aggressive and harder to control, 29% said they were resentful and embittered and 21% said that their children lacked respect for them.

- Almost a third said their children had low self-esteem, and 24% thought their children had problems trusting people and forming relationships.
- Many (77%) of the mothers no longer lived in the violent relationship. One worrying statistic was that 23% of the mothers left because their partner had begun to hit their children.
- Almost three-quarters of the mothers had found it difficult to talk to professionals about their children's problems because they feared that their children would be taken away from them.

Leaving was a major upheaval for both mothers and children. Over 60% had to find a new GP, 48% of children changed schools and most mothers and children had to find new friends. It would be more preferable if services were geared to removing the abuser from the family home rather than the mother and children.

Source: *The Hidden Victims – children and domestic violence.* NCH Action For Children, 1994.

A more recent British Medical Association (BMA) report on domestic violence has confirmed many of NCH's findings about the impact of domestic violence on children. It concluded that witnessing domestic violence can cause considerable harm to children in both the short and long term.

In the short term children may show a range of disturbed behaviour including withdrawal, depression, increased aggression, fear and anxiety. Boys are more likely to show increased aggression in the longer term and many children may suffer post-traumatic stress disorder.

Children who witness domestic violence may blame themselves for it happening, or take on responsibility to protect the mother and/or siblings. Children may feel guilty that they were unable to protect their mothers or stop the violence from happening. Where there is domestic violence to the mother there is an increased risk that there will be violence to the child as well.

Source: *Domestic Violence: a health care issue?*
British Medical Association, 1998.

Looked after children/children in care

Under the Children Act 1989 in England and Wales, a child or young person is 'looked after' by a local authority if she or he is placed in their care by a court (under a care order) or provided with accommodation by the authority's social services department for more than 24 hours.

Numbers of children looked after in England

At 31 March 1999 local authorities in England were looking after 55,300 children, 30,100 (55%) boys and 25,100 (45%) girls. This was a 4% increase on the previous year's figures and represents a rate of 49 per 10,000 children under 18 years of age. Following a fall from almost 100,000 in the early 1980s to 49,100 in 1994, the looked after population has been steadily rising again.

The numbers of children entering and leaving the looked after children system have been falling since the mid-1990s. During 1998–99, 28,300 children started to be looked after and 26,900 children ceased to be looked after. These figures represent falls of 5% and 8% respectively, compared to the previous year.

The increase in the total is due to the fact that, overall, children are spending longer being looked after: following a dip in the mid-1990s, the average length of the latest period of care has increased by 9% from 17½ months in 1996 to 19 months in 1999, returning to around the same level as the early 1990s. A more detailed analysis reveals that the looked after population is divided between those experiencing rapid turnover and children who stay longer. In 1998–99, 40% of children leaving care in that year had been looked after for eight weeks or less, 22% had been looked after for more than two years and 7% for more than five years. About 40% of all children looked after on 31 March 1999 had been in care for three years or more.

A child who has been in care for more than six months has a 60% chance of remaining in care for four years or more (and most likely until leaving the system at 16 years of age). By 12 months this has risen to almost 80%.

The looked after population is becoming younger. The average age has fallen from 11 years 3 months in 1994 to 10 years 4 months in 1999. Over the same period there has been a 49% increase in the number of looked after children under one, and a 45% increase in the numbers aged 1–4, compared to the overall increase of 13%.

Sources: *Children Looked After by Local Authorities,* Department of Health, 1999; *Prime Minister's Review of Adoption, a Performance and Innovation Unit report,* Cabinet Office, 2000.

Placements of looked after children in England

There were 36,100 (65%) looked after children in foster placements at 31 March 1999. This proportion has increased by 3% since 1995. About 6,300 children were looked after in children's homes, 4,800 of whom were in local authority-run community homes.

The figure of 6,300 represents an increase of about 100 on the previous year, against a context in which there has been an increase in the number of privately registered children's homes.

There were 6,200 (11%) looked after children placed with their parents at 31 March 1999, compared to 9% in 1995.

Table 5.1: Children looked after by placement at 31 March 1999, England.

	1995	1998	1999
All children[1]	49,800	53,300	55,300
Foster placements	32,100	35,100	36,100
Children's homes of which:	7,200	6,200	6,300
Community homes	5,900	4,900	4,800
Voluntary homes and hostels	580	550	500
Private registered children's homes	780	770	1,000
Schools and associated homes and hostels	920	970	1,000
Placed with parents	4,400	5,600	6,200
Placed for adoption in lodgings, residential	2,200	2,500	2,900
Employment or living independently	1,400	1,200	1,200
Other placement	1,600	1,800	1,600

1 Figures for children looked after exclude agreed series of short-term placements.

Source: *Children Looked After by Local Authorities, Year ending 31 March 1999, England*, Department of Health, 2000.

Legal status of looked after children in England

At 31 March 1999, 34,100 children were looked after under a care order, over 2,000 more than a year earlier. The number of interim (often emergency) care orders is up by 92% while the number under voluntary agreements is down by 4%, compared with 1995.

Table 5.2: Numbers of children looked after by legal status at 31 March 1999, England.

	1999
All children[1]	55,300
Care orders	34,100
Of which: interim	7,100
full[2]	27,000
Voluntary arrangements under Sec 20 CA 1989[3]	18,800
Freed for adoption	1,300
Other[4]	1,100

1 Figures for children looked after in this table exclude agreed series of short-term placements.
2 Includes deemed care orders.
3 Single occasion, not part of a series of short-term placements.
4 Includes children on remand, committed for trial or detained, and children subject to emergency orders or police protection. Also includes c.130 children subject to compulsory order under section 53 of the CYPA 1933, who are technically not looked after.

Source: *Children Looked After by Local Authorities, Year ending 31 March 1999, England*, Department of Health, 2000.

Reasons for children starting to be looked after

Table 5.3: Children who started to be looked after, by reason[1].

	1995	1998	1999
All children[2]	32,400	29,700	28,400
No parents	330	420	570
Abandoned or lost	850	930	1,000
Family or child homeless	470	300	380
Parent(s) in prison	360	340	380
Breakdown of adoptive family	50	50	50
Preliminary to adoption	500	460	430
Parent's health	4,300	3,700	3,100
Parents/families need of relief			
– child with disabilities	720	360	460
– other	8,500	7,400	6,000
Abuse or neglect	6,200	7,800	8,300
Concern for child's welfare	3,100	2,300	2,400
Own behaviour	1,800	1,400	1,300
Accused or guilty of an offence	1,600	1,800	1,700
At request of child	1,100	760	650
Other	2,500	1,700	1,600

1 Only the first occasion on which a child started to be looked after in the year has been counted.

2 Figures for children looked after in this table exclude agreed series of short-term placements.

Source: *Children Looked After by Local Authorities, Year ending 31 March 1999, England*, Department of Health, 2000.

There are indications that the needs of those looked after are becoming more challenging. Between 1995 and 1999 there was a 53% increase in the proportion of children starting to be looked after because of abuse or neglect, up from 19% to 29%. This is mirrored by the increase in the proportion of children coming into care under Care Orders or Emergency Protection Orders, referred to above.

Source: *Prime Minister's Review of Adoption, a Performance and Innovation Unit report*, Cabinet Office, 2000.

Children looked after in Wales

At 31 March 1998 there were 3,033 children looked after by local authorities in Wales, 1,687 boys and 1,346 girls. Since the 1980s the number of children looked after in Wales has fallen from nearly 5,000 to 3,300 in 1990, and has remained at about the same level since.

Foster placements account for 69% of all placements compared with 35% in 1980. Only 6% of children are now accommodated in residential homes and the number of local authority homes has fallen from 123 in 1980 to 32 in 1998.

Source: *Social Services Statistics Wales 1999*, Government Statistical Service, Welsh Office, 1999.

Table 5.4: Children looked after in Wales by placement, 1998.

	1980	1990	1994	1997	1998
Foster placements	1,709	1,994	1,973	2,303	2,340
Community homes	1,445	569	330	232	200
Voluntary homes	153	16	23	5	3
With parents or family	1,207	451	396	289	273
Placed for Adoption	–	60	87	93	87
Independent accommodation	88	82	136	106	83
Absent, other	259	106	88	262	414
Total	**4,861**	**3,278**	**3,033**	**3,290**	**3,400**

Source: *Social Services Statistics Wales 1999*, Government Statistical Service, Welsh Office, 1999.

Leaving care

Table 5.5: Children aged 16 and over who ceased to be looked after[1], England.

	1995	1998	1999
All children[2]	8,700	7,700	7,100
Sex			
Boys	4,500	4,200	4,000
Girls	4,200	3,500	3,100
Age on leaving care			
16	3,400	3,500	3,400
17	1,400	1,400	1,400
18th birthday	3,800	2,800	2,200
Older than 18th birthday	150	140	80
Final placement			
Foster placement	3,600	3,600	3,300
Children's homes[3]	2,100	1,800	1,500
Living independently[4]	1,900	1,300	1,300
Placed with parents	490	490	420
Other	740	600	650
Duration of final period of care[5]			
Under 6 months	2,300	2,000	1,800
6 mths to under 1 year	910	750	640
1 year to under 2 years	1,400	1,100	1,000
2 years and over	4,200	3,900	3,700

1 Only the latest occasion on which a child ceased to be looked after in the year has been counted.
2 Figures for children looked after in this table exclude agreed series of short-term placements.
3 Includes community homes, voluntary homes and hostels, and private registered children's homes.
4 Includes living in lodgings, living independently, and in residential employment.
5 'Period of care' refers to a continuous period of being looked after, which may indicate more than one placement or legal status.

Source: *Children Looked After by Local Authorities, Year ending 31 March 1999, England,* Department of Health, 2000.

In 1999, 7,100 young people left care. The numbers leaving care have been falling steadily since 1993. There were 3,400 (47%) care leavers aged 16, a proportion that has increased since 1993. The Government is concerned that some young people are discharged from care at 16 for reasons related more to cost than to the young people's best interests and have recently introduced measures to deter this. If these disincentives are effective we may expect the proportion of young people leaving care at 17 and above to increase in future years.

Being looked after: outcomes

The outcomes related to having been looked after are almost uniformly poor, although some resilient young people manage to overcome the disadvantage that attaches to having a care background and do very well. Research demonstrates the following:

- Education: more than 75% of care leavers have no educational qualifications; fewer than 20% continue in full-time education after 16; there are high levels of non-attendance and exclusion from school among looked after children.
- Employment: between 50% and 80% of care leavers are unemployed. The Who Cares? Trust found that many employers said they would be reluctant to employ care leavers.
- Offending: 23% of adult prisoners and 38% of young prisoners have been in care.

- Health: Nearly half the young people in a Save the Children Fund survey found leaving care affected their health, mostly adversely and in terms of their diet and mental health. Forty-two per cent said they were not eating enough.
- Parenthood: at least 1 in 7 young women leaving care are pregnant or mothers.
- Housing: The Save the Children survey found that 47% of care leavers moved into their own flat or bedsit; over a quarter (27%) moved into supported accommodation or a hostel; others went to the family home or friends. A third had received no help in finding housing and had to deal with it themselves. Over 84% had moved home at least once since leaving care; many moved three (10%) or four (16%) times. Nearly all (93%) were living in rented accommodation, with half in housing association and a quarter in council housing. Nearly a half did not receive a leaving care grant: for others the amount varied from £5 to £1,800.
- Homelessness: young people who have been looked after are greatly over-represented in the numbers of homeless young people. Having left care, many young people are unable to cope with the isolation and practical demands of living on their own. Various studies have found between a quarter and a third of the young homeless have been in care. Young people with care backgrounds are 60 times more likely to be homeless than others. Forty per cent of homeless people using Centrepoint's services in London and an estimated 28% of young homeless people outside London have been in care.

- Poverty: 1 in 10 16–17-year-old claimants of DSS severe hardship payments have been in care. According to Save the Children, 81% of the care leavers interviewed said their income was not enough to live on. Nearly 80% had faced circumstances where they had no money. The majority were on benefits and unemployed.
- Unemployment: young people who have been looked after are four times more likely than others to be unemployed.
- Support: The Save the Children research found that 40% of the young people had no support at all after leaving care. There was a significant difference in receiving support between young Black and young White care leavers.

Sources: *Too Much Too Young*, Action on Aftercare Consortium, 1996; *You're On Your Own*, Save the Children, 1995; *Strategic Planning in Children's Services*, Department of Health, 1999.

The Children (Leaving Care) Act 2000, once implemented, and the Quality Protects programme should gradually impact on the adverse outcomes reported above.

Adoption

The total numbers of adoptions in England have fallen from about 20,000 per year in 1970 to 4,100 in 1999. This principally reflects the sharp reduction in the number of babies of unmarried mothers given up for adoption, driven by the decrease in stigma associated with illegitimacy and single motherhood, and increased access to contraception and abortion.

In 1998–99, 2,200 children were adopted from a total of 55,300 children looked after by local authorities, a rate of 4%. This proportion is now stable, after a dip in the mid-1990s.

In the same year 2,900 children were placed with carers with a view to adoption at a future date, 5.2% of the total of looked after children.

Source: *Prime Minister's Review of Adoption, a Performance and Innovation Unit report*, Cabinet Office, 2000.

The profile of children adopted from care

The following is drawn from the *Prime Minister's Review of Adoption*, carried out by the Performance and Innovation Unit in the Cabinet Office and published in July 2000.

Children currently adopted from care form a distinct subset of looked after children. Compared with the overall looked after population they:

- Are more likely to be female and White: 49% of the adopted children were girls although girls comprise only 45% of the looked after population; 90% were White, while White children make up 83% of the total population.
- Are likely to be part of sibling groups but placed apart.
- Are becoming younger and have an average age lower than that of the looked after population: the average age of adopted children from care is five years nine months and relatively few children over ten are adopted.

- Enter care at a younger age than the general looked after population.
- Are more challenging than the general looked after population: 1996 figures suggest that 44% of children adopted from care had started to be looked after because of abuse, neglect or risk, compared to 17% of the overall number of children ceasing to be looked after that year.
- Spend years in care before adoption, but this time is falling: length of time in care before adoption was on average two years and ten months in 1999.
- Wait to be placed for adoption, but this time is falling: from one year eleven months in 1994 to one year eight months in 1998–99.
- Are unlikely to have returned home before adoption.
- Experience more moves while in care.

The conclusions drawn from this data by the Performance and Innovation Unit included the following:

- Adoption has changed radically over the last 30 years.
- Adoption from care is not about providing couples with trouble-free babies. It is about finding families for children of a range of ages, with challenging backgrounds and complex needs.
- This means that promoting adoption will involve finding more families for increasingly vulnerable children.

- There is evidence to suggest that the process of deciding on adoption is lengthy and that children would benefit from more timely decision making.
- Research[1] shows that the best outcomes are achieved from placing children for adoption at a young age, so there is a balance to be struck between appropriate attempts at rehabilitation with birth families and avoiding drift and delay which damage the child.

1 *What works in child and family placement?*, Sellick and Thoburn, British Association for Adoption and Fostering, 1996.

Is the relatively low level of adoption from care due to social workers' hostility?

The following paragraph is of note in the Performance and Innovation Unit's comprehensive report:

> "Some commentators have suggested that these problems (the relatively low level of adoptions of children from care) are the result of social workers' hostility to adoption. While there can be issues at an individual level, the study found little evidence of an institutional anti-adoption culture in social service departments. The more likely explanation for the limited use of adoption, on the basis of our visits and consultations, is that both social workers and their direct managers are (properly) highly committed to working to reunite children with their birth parents and the structures and procedures are not in place to ensure they think more widely than that. Social workers are also relatively untrained and inexperienced in adoption work."

Source: paragraph 3.33, *Prime Minister's Review of Adoption, a Performance and Innovation Unit report*, Cabinet Office, 2000.

Adoption: international comparisons

Unpublished research[1] included in the Performance and Innovation Unit's report shows that the percentage of children adopted from care in the industrialised countries varies from 6.6% in the USA at the highest, to 0.2% in Sweden, the lowest. In England the rate is 4%, the second highest.

1 University of Bristol, April 2000, for the Performance and Innovation Unit study.

These differences reflect the different priority given to adoption in each country. The UK is closer to the USA in the extent to which it is prepared to overrule parental wishes in order to place children for adoption. Elsewhere, particularly in Europe, there is much greater reluctance to overrule the wishes of parents.

In the USA, legislation was passed in 1997 to encourage the adoption of greater numbers of children in care. The Adoption and Safe Families Act 1997 shortened the timeframes for conducting permanency hearings and created a new requirement for states to make 'reasonable efforts' to finalise permanent placements and establish timeframes in which to file petitions for the termination of parental rights for certain children in care.

Source: *Prime Minister's Review of Adoption, a Performance and Innovation Unit report*, Cabinet Office, 2000.

Health

Infant mortality

During this century there have been dramatic improvements in both infant and childhood mortality in England and Wales. Mortality rates are generally at their highest immediately after birth. They fall sharply throughout the first year of life and continue to fall, though more slowly, to a minimum in the five to nine age group. The rates then rise gradually with age. At all ages in infancy and childhood, mortality rates are higher for boys than girls.

Many factors are linked with the chances of a baby dying before its first birthday. These include birth weight, number of babies born to the mother at the same time, age of the mother, social class of the father and ethnicity.

The infant mortality rate (the number of babies dying under one year of age per 1,000 live births) in England and Wales in 1998 was 5.7, a decline from 6.1 in 1996. The rate has fallen steadily since 1986 when there were 9.6 deaths per 1,000 live births. In 1900–02, the rate was 142 deaths per 1,000 live births.

Neonatal deaths (deaths at ages less than 28 days) have also fallen at a steady rate and in 1998 the neonatal death rate in England and Wales was 3.8.

Declines in infant mortality have contributed greatly to improvements in overall life expectancy at birth. In 1997, life expectancy at birth in the UK was approaching 75 years for males and 80 for females, compared with just over 50 years for men and 54 years for women in 1911.

Sources: *Mortality Statistics*, ONS, The Stationery Office, 1999; *Social Trends 30*, ONS, The Stationery Office, 2000.

Infant mortality: variations by ethnicity

Ethnicity is not collected on birth registration forms, but the country of birth of the mother is. Although this is an imperfect proxy measure for ethnicity, it does give some insight into differences in infant mortality rates for those whose mothers are born outside the UK and who then migrated here. Overall, babies born in England and Wales in 1998 whose mothers were born outside the UK had a higher risk of dying by their first birthday. However, the risks were not the same for every country of birth of the mother. Babies born to mothers born in Pakistan or the Caribbean were more than twice as likely to die when infants than the majority of babies – those whose mothers were born in the UK.

Source: *Social Inequalities*, ONS, The Stationery Office, 2000.

Infant mortality: variations by class

Despite the improvement in the overall infant mortality rate, big differences still remain between the social classes. For babies born inside marriage in 1997, the infant mortality rate for those whose fathers were unskilled was one and a half times higher than that for those whose fathers were in the professional social class. For babies born outside marriage, the mortality rate was 6.9 deaths per thousand live births, compared with 5.2 deaths per 1,000 live births for those born inside marriage. There have, however, been large increases in the proportions of babies born outside marriage for all social classes.

Many of these births are jointly registered, reflecting the increase in cohabitation. Although infant mortality rates in each class have decreased over the last decade or so, there is no evidence that the class differential has decreased over this period.

Table 6.1: Infant mortality[1] by social class[2], United Kingdom.

Rates per 1,000 live births	1981	1991	1997
Inside marriage:			
Professional	7.8	5.0	4.4
Managerial and technical	8.2	5.3	4.0
Skilled non-manual	9.0	6.2	5.4
Skilled manual	10.5	6.3	5.3
Semi-skilled	12.7	7.2	6.4
Unskilled	15.7	8.4	6.8
Other	15.6	11.8	8.8
All inside marriage	**10.4**	**6.3**	**5.2**
Outside marriage:			
Joint registration	14.1	8.7	6.8
Sole registration	16.2	10.8	7.3
All outside marriage	**15.0**	**9.3**	**6.9**

1 Deaths within one year.
2 Based on occupation of father.

Source: *Social Trends 30*, ONS, The Stationery Office, 2000.

Childhood mortality

Childhood mortality rates have been falling steadily in England and Wales for over 100 years. The most marked long-term decrease in mortality has been among the youngest children, those aged 1 to 4 years. The total number of childhood deaths (1–15-years-old) in 1996 was 1,841. As with previous years, injury and poisoning was the major cause of death for children aged 1–15 in 1996.

Apart from infancy, death rates among children and young people are highest in the 15–19 year age group. This is primarily because of the increase in injury and poisoning, and in transport accidents.

Sources: *Mortality Statistics*, ONS, The Stationery Office, 1998; *Key Data on Adolescence*, J Coleman, Trust For The Study Of Adolescence, 1999.

Childhood mortality: international comparisons

While childhood deaths in the UK have been falling, they are still high in comparison with other countries in Europe. The UK ranks 18th in a league table of deaths in early childhood, behind countries that include Slovenia and Singapore as well as France and Germany. The UK's death rate of seven per 1,000 births under five, most from accidents, is 75% higher than the Scandinavian rate.

A report by the BMA shows that among the British children who do not survive beyond the age of four, 22% die from injury or poisoning, 20% from birth abnormalities, 13% from cancer and 12% from diseases of the nervous system.

Table 6.2: Childhood mortality rates by country.

Ranking	Country	Mortality per 1,000 live births in children under 5
1	Sweden	4
1	Singapore	4
1	Finland	4
4	Switzerland	5
4	Spain	5
4	Iceland	5
7	Slovenia	6
7	Norway	6
7	Netherlands	6
7	Monaco	6
7	Japan	6
7	Germany	6
7	France	6
7	Denmark	6
7	Austria	6
7	Australia	6
7	Andorra	6
18	**UK**	**7**
18	Ireland	7
18	New Zealand	7
29	USA	8
43	Chile	13
99	Philippines	38
109	Turkey	47
146	India	111
159	Pakistan	136
191	Niger	320

Source: *Growing Up In Britain*, British Medical Association, 1999.

Childhood morbidity (illness and disability)

Although death rates have fallen and life expectancy has increased, there is little evidence that the population is experiencing less morbidity than 10 or 20 years ago. There has been a slight increase in self-reported long-standing illness and limiting long-standing illness, and socio-economic differences are substantial. According to a British Medical Association report, children in the lowest income level (Social Class V) have nearly twice the rate of long-standing illness than those in Social Class 1.

Source: *Growing Up In Britain*, British Medical Association, 1999.

The 1997 *Health Survey for England* focused on the health of children and young adults aged 2–24. It found that the proportion reporting a long-standing illness, disability or infirmity that had troubled them was higher among boys aged 2–15 (26%) than girls aged 2–15 (22%), but higher for young women aged 16–24 (27%) than young men aged 16–24 (23%). The proportion reporting a long-standing illness that limited their activities in some way was 10% for boys, 9% for girls, 11% for young men and 13% for young women. The proportion reporting good or very good health was relatively low in manual social classes and in households with lower incomes.

Source: *Health Survey for England: The Health of Young People 95–97*, Department of Health, 1998.

Asthma

Asthma is now the most common chronic childhood disease in Britain and its prevalence is rising. In England the prevalence of doctor-diagnosed asthma is higher among young males than young females. Between 1995 and 1997 23% of males and 18% of females aged 2–15 reported a diagnosis of asthma made by a doctor. The variation in the diagnosis by gender decreases with age so that in the 20–24 age groups there was no difference at all.

Social Trends 30, ONS, The Stationery Office, 2000.

Childhood accidents

There are no absolute statistics available for injuries sustained in accidents. The Child Accident Prevention Trust report that 2.5 million is a reasonable estimate for the number of attendances at accident and emergency units each year. Indeed, children have two in five of all home and leisure accidents seen in UK hospitals.

According to the *Health Survey for England 1997*, the estimated annual accident rate for boys is around 31 major accidents and 216 minor accidents per 100 boys aged under 16, while for girls it is 22 major accidents and 144 minor accidents per 100. For young men aged 16–24 the estimated accident rate was 42 major accidents and 385 minor accidents per 100 and for young women aged 16–24 it was 22 major accidents and 184 minor accidents per 100.

Accident rates varied with age. For males, the major accident rate for those aged 12 to 24 was around twice that for those aged 2–11. The accident rate for females peaked between the ages of 11 and 15.

Source: *Health Survey for England: The Health of Young People 95–97*, Department of Health, 1998.

The British Medical Association has reported that children in Social Class V (manual) are four times more likely to die in an accident than those in Social Class 1 (professional). This may be principally because children growing up in families on low incomes tend to play in busy streets and in dangerous areas of the home such as kitchens.

Source: *Growing Up In Britain*, British Medical Association, 1999.

Children and young people's mental health

About 10% of children aged 5 to 15 in Great Britain in 1998 have a mental disorder[1] of sufficient severity as to cause them distress or have a considerable effect on the way they live.

1 Mental disorder defined as including emotional problems – anxiety or depression, conduct – awkward, troublesome, aggressive or anti-social behaviour, hyperkinetic – shown by inattention and overactivity. The criteria used to assess disorder were: a clinically recognisable set of symptoms, behaviour associated with considerable distress and substantial interference with personal functions.

Source: *Mental Health of Children and Adolescents*, ONS, 1999, reported in *Social Inequalities*, ONS, 2000.

Overall figures from epidemiological studies of children and adolescents spanning years 4 to 20 suggest that diagnosable anxiety disorders affect around 12% of this age range, disruptive disorders around 10%, attention deficit disorder 5%, and specific developmental disorders, enuresis and substance abuse up to 6%, depending on age group. Psychotic and pervasive developmental disorders, such as autistic disorder, are very rare, affecting less than 1%.

It is estimated that at least 50% and possibly as many as 100% of children with more severe mental health disorders are affected for many years after the initial diagnosis. Disorders with a particularly poor outcome include pervasive developmental disorders, childhood schizophrenia and attention deficit hyperactivity disorder. Whilst there is some disagreement concerning the overall prevalence rate for child and adolescent mental health problems in the UK, there is a consensus that rates of recorded problems are rising.

Source: *Bright Futures: Promoting children and young people's mental health,* The Mental Health Foundation, 1999.

Approximately 10% of children and young people have mental health problems that are severe enough to require professional help. A typical health district may have between 5,000 and 12,000 children with mental health problems that require psychiatric help.

Source: *The Fundamental Facts . . . all the latest facts and figures on mental illness,* Mental Health Foundation, 1999.

Risk factors concerning the development of children's mental health problems

The risk factors set out below are those believed to increase the probability of a child developing mental health problems. They are cumulative: if a child has only one risk factor in their life, their probability of developing a mental health problem is between 1% and 2%, with three risk factors the likelihood increases to 8% and with four or more risk factors the likelihood of the child developing a mental health problem is increased by 20%.

Table 6.3: Risk factors for mental ill-health in children.

In the child	In the family
Genetic influences	Overt parental conflict
Low IQ and learning disability	Family breakdown
Specific developmental delay	Inconsistent or unclear discipline
Communication difficulty	Hostile and rejecting relationships
Difficult temperament	Failure to adapt to child's changing needs
Physical illness especially if chronic and/or neurological	Parental criminality, alcoholism or personality disorder
Academic failure	Physical, sexual and/or emotional abuse
Low self-esteem	Parental psychiatric illness
	Death and loss – including loss of friendship

Continued opposite.

Table 6.3: Continued.

In the community	
Socio-economic disadvantage	Homelessness
Disaster	Discrimination
Other significant life events	

Source: *Bright Futures: Promoting children and young people's mental health,* The Mental Health Foundation, 1999.

Children's mental health problems and family income

There have been shown to be strong links between family income and the mental health of children. In households where the gross weekly income was under £200, 16% of children aged 5–15 had some kind of disorder – emotional, conduct or hyperkinetic. The percentage was lower among households with higher weekly incomes: in households with over £500 per week about 6% of children had a mental disorder.

Source: *Mental Health of Children and Adolescents,* ONS, 1999, reported in *Social Inequalities,* ONS, 2000.

Eating disorders

Anorexia nervosa: This is where a person seeks to maintain or reduce their body weight by controlling their calorie intake and is often associated with a distorted perception of body image and low self-esteem. It has been classified as a 'severe psychiatric disorder', due to the likelihood of long-term disability and the high mortality rate. It is currently the third most 'chronic illness' in teenage girls and the rate is rising.

One per cent of women in the UK between the ages of 15–30 years have anorexia nervosa. Fifty per cent of cases will occur before the age of 20. The ratio of males to females is around 1:12. Anorexia nervosa usually persists for about six years. Unlike other forms of mental health problems, the hospital admission rates for anorexia nervosa have risen over the last two decades. Although in-patient care is thought to be successful in the short term, the likelihood of relapse is high.

Bulimia nervosa: This is characterised by a need to maintain body weight through a chaotic cycle of bingeing followed by purging or excessive exercise and fasting. An estimated 1–2% of adult women in the UK have bulimia nervosa. Compared with anorexia, women with bulimia tend to be older. Some men experience bulimia nervosa, although it is less common than among women.

Source: *The Fundamental Facts . . . all the latest facts and figures on mental illness*, The Mental Health Foundation, 1999.

Suicide

In 1999, 3,685 deaths in England and Wales were registered as having been caused by suicide, 2,856 of them to men and 829 of them to women. Two of these suicides were by boys aged 5–14. There were 348 suicides by young people aged 15–24: 279 by young men and 69 by young women.

Source: *Health Statistics Quarterly Report*, ONS, 1999.

In the UK there has been a marked increase in the suicide rate in people aged 15–24 since the end of the 1950s. Between 1971 and 1997 the suicide rate for men aged 15–24 rose from 6.9 per 10,000 population to 16.4 per 10,000 population. Conversely, for women in this age group there was a fall from the mid-1970s to the mid-1980s. The rate was 4.0 per 10,000 population in 1997.

Source: *Social Trends 30*, ONS, The Stationery Office, 2000.

Suicide accounts for 20% of all deaths by young people. In young people who commit suicide 3 in 5 will have experienced 'emotional and behavioural difficulties' for several months prior to the attempt. Young people who have a friend or relative who has harmed or killed themselves are at greater risk of suicide. A third of adolescents who kill themselves have a history of previous attempts.

Sources: *The Fundamental Facts . . . all the latest facts and figures on mental illness*, The Mental Health Foundation, 1999; *Key Data on Adolescence*, J Coleman, Trust for the Study of Adolescence, 1999.

Self-harm

'Self-harm' describes all acts of self-harm, self-injury and attempted suicide. Statistics for self-harm are generally unreliable, as it is often hidden and unreported.

- Approximately 142,000 hospital admissions each year in England and Wales are due to self-harm, mainly self-injury and drug overdoses, about 19,000 of them to young people.

- One in ten adolescents who have deliberately harmed themselves will do so on more than one occasion.
- Adolescents who self-harm are more at risk of developing 'mental disorders' and 'personality disturbance' in later life, including behavioural problems and 'major affective disorders'. There is often a background of abuse and family dysfunction.
- A survey of women who self-injured found that 90% had cut themselves, a third had inflicted blows or scalded themselves; 74% had begun self-injuring during childhood or adolescence (0–19 years) and 69% had been inflicting injuries on themselves for more than five years.

Source: *The Fundamental Facts . . . all the latest facts and figures on mental illness*, The Mental Health Foundation, 1999.

Diet, lifestyle and body image

Government research published in 2000 showed that children are eating too much junk food and not taking enough exercise, storing up serious health problems for themselves in the future. Levels of fruit and vegetable consumption were low, especially among children from lower socio-economic groups. More generally, the study showed that these children had much worse diets, were fatter and did less exercise than children with parents in non-manual or professional occupations.

The survey showed that 40% of boys and 60% of girls were spending, on average, less than one hour a day doing physically intense activities. For every 25g of leafy green vegetables the children ate they consumed an average of 100g of sweets and chocolate. The study also showed that 16% of girls aged 15 to 18 were dieting to lose weight.

Source: *The National Diet and Nutrition Survey of Young People aged 4–18*, Department of Health and Food Standards Agency, The Stationery Office, 2000.

A survey published this year bears out the fact that many young women are concerned about their body image. Some 23% of 13–15-year-olds said they thought they were too heavy, rising to 28% among 16–19-year-olds and 38% of 20–24-year-olds. In contrast, more than half of all boys said they thought they were the right weight.

Source: *Health Survey for England,* Department of Health, 2000.

Substance misuse: a caveat about comparing research findings

Ascertaining the true extent of substance misuse in children and young people is very difficult. Responses to surveys often rely upon self-report questionnaires, which may lead to answers being overstated through bravado, or understated through wariness. Surveys which are school-based do not necessarily include those who have 'dropped out', a group at high risk of misusing alcohol and drugs. Drugs misuse by young people also seems to vary in type and seriousness by area, so the geographical focus of studies is likely to be an important determinant of their results.

Children and smoking

One in nine 11–15-year-olds and 1 in 3 16–19-year-olds smoke regularly in Great Britain.

Source: *Smoking, drinking and drug use among young teenagers in 1998*, ONS, The Stationery Office, 1999.

Research has shown that there are relatively low levels of cigarette smoking among young people in households in Social Class 1 and high levels among those in households in Social Class V. Children aged 13–15 are more likely to smoke in households where at least one adult smokes (24%) than in those in which no adult smokes (7%).

Source: *Health Survey for England: The Health of Young People 1995–7*, Department of Health, 1998.

Children and young people and alcohol

A Government survey of children aged 11–16 found the majority said they had tasted an alcoholic drink. The proportion saying they had done so increased from 77% of children in Year 7 to 93% of those in Year 9, to virtually all (96%) in Year 11. In all years, similar proportions of boys and girls had tasted alcohol. Nineteen per cent of the young people said they did not currently drink alcohol, 15% said they drank a moderate amount and 7% that they drank more than this. Alcoholic soft drinks (alcopops) were most popular: 18% of those drinking alcohol said they drank this type of drink at least once a week. Next in popularity was cider (14% at least once a week), followed by normal strength lager (12%) and spirits/liqueurs/cocktails (12%). Just over

1 in 5 (22%) had been really drunk once and nearly two-fifths (39%) up to three times. A further 9% had been really drunk between four and ten times and 1 in 10 drinkers had been really drunk more than 10 times. One in five (20%) of Year 11 drinkers had been drunk more than ten times.

Source: *Young people and health: health behaviour in school-aged children,* Health Education Authority, 1999.

A report published in May 2000 suggested a worrying trend in binge drinking among young people, with 37% of young men and 23% of young women aged 16 to 24 regularly drinking twice the recommended daily limits. Eleven to fifteen-year-olds were also reported to be drinking more, with their average weekly consumption nearly doubling between 1990 and 1998 from 5.3 to 9.9 units. Doctors blamed this increase in teenage drinking largely on alcopops.

Source: *Britain's Ruin,* Alcohol Concern, 2000.

Research published by the European Commission found that boys in Wales were the most likely in Europe to report drunkenness, with seven out of ten 15-year-olds saying they had been drunk at least twice. Britain was one of the EU states in which the frequency of drinking among young people was found to be increasing.

Source: *Report on the state of young people's health in the EU: a Commission Services working paper,* Directorate General for Health and Consumer Protection, European Commission, 2000.

Children and young people and drugs misuse

The Exeter Schools Health Education Unit regularly carries out a health-related behaviour survey of more than 40,000 children in schools. Their 1999 survey found that:

- 39% of 14–15-year-olds know where to obtain an illegal drug and 58% are fairly sure or certain that they know a drug user.
- 44% of 14–15-year-olds have been offered an illegal drug at some time.
- 21% of 14–15-year-olds have tried an illegal drug at some time.
- These latest figures suggest that the percentage of young people who have tried an illegal drug at least once rose steadily from the first survey in 1987, peaked in 1995–96 and has stabilised, or possibly even come down, since then.

Source: *Young People and Illegal Drugs in 1999*, Balding J., Schools Health Education Unit, 2000.

A longer-term review of drugs misuse by young people shows that its prevalence among 12–13-year-olds has increased fivefold and among 14–15-year-olds eightfold since 1987.

Source: *Young People and Drugs*, SCODA and Children's Legal Centre, 1999.

In 1998 the *British Crime Survey* found that 29% of 16–24-year-olds in England and Wales had used an illegal drug during the last year and 19% had done so during the last month. Cannabis was the most frequently used drug, followed by amphetamines and ecstasy.

Although only 3% reported using cocaine in the last year there had been a significant increase in the proportions using this drug since 1996. Use of cocaine was more apparent in London, the South and Merseyside than elsewhere in England and Wales.

Source: *British Crime Survey*, Home Office, 1998, reported in *Social Trends 30*, ONS, The Stationery Office, 2000.

Four out of ten British 15 and 16-year-olds have smoked cannabis, more than in any other country in the EU, including Holland where cannabis is legal. More 15 and 16-year-olds use speed, hallucinogens and ecstasy in Britain, Ireland and Holland, compared to other EU countries.

Source: The European Monitoring Centre for Drugs and Drug Addiction, 1999.

Research into young people's health across the EU, published after the drugs research cited above, endorsed its findings and also found that amphetamines have been tried by 13% of young people in England and Wales, compared with 8% in Holland and fewer than 4% in other EU countries. Ireland had the most ecstasy users in the 15–16 age group, followed by England, Wales and Holland – the only EU countries where use of this 'dance drug' borders on 10%. Elsewhere, the drug registered below 5% and barely figured at all in Scandinavia and Portugal.

Source: *Report on the state of young people's health in the EU: a Commission Services working paper*, Directorate General for Health and Consumer Protection, European Commission, 2000.

Research focusing on heroin use by young people in the North of England found that 5–20% had been given the opportunity to try heroin by friends or dealers. Small cities and towns were reported to be the current sites of heroin outbreaks, rather than the major cities. The average young heroin addict was smoking cigarettes at 11, drinking alcohol at 12, smoking cannabis at 13 and trying heroin by 15. Most were out of parental control by the age of 13. Two in three had experienced family breakdown or some other traumatic life event during childhood. Once they had tried heroin they had built up rapidly to higher doses before developing a repertoire of drug use, including crack cocaine, tranquillisers and the heroin substitute methadone.

More than half said they could get hold of heroin 24 hours a day. Daily heroin users had an average drugs bill of £206 per week. Hardly any of the young people were in employment and two-thirds were in receipt of benefits. Half the teenagers, half of whom were girls, had become involved in crime before they became heroin users, but the drug had intensified their offending. Shoplifting was the dominant offence committed, but a significant minority of the young men were dealing in drugs and begging and prostitution were other means of raising money.

Source: *Hidden Heroin Users,* Parker H., Drugscope, 2000.

A report published by *Face* magazine suggests that drugs misuse varies significantly by region across the UK. Consumption of magic mushrooms was highest in Wales, where 19% of 15–16-year-olds were reported to use them. In Sheffield, over a third of children were reported to have tried at least one illicit drug by the time they were 14. In Nottingham, among Asian people aged under 25, 86% were reported to have used cannabis, more than admitted drinking alcohol (83%). In London, use of opiates and cocaine was three times the national average with nearly 1 in 10 16–29-year-olds saying they had taken opiates in the last year.

Source: Research for *Face* magazine, *"Revealed: a map of drug-taking across Britain"*, in the *Independent* newspaper, 11/12/1999.

Volatile substance abuse

Glue sniffing first became popular among young people in the mid-1970s. Since that time, the number of different substances inhaled has increased to include the misuse of glues, gas fuels, aerosols and other volatile substances. Estimates of the extent of volatile substance abuse by young people in Britain vary, but in 2000 the EU reported that 1 in 5 15–16-year-olds in Britain abuses solvents. In Austria and Portugal volatile substance abuse was reported to be 'unheard of'.

Conversely, the 1999 Exeter Schools Health Education Unit survey found that only 3–4% of 14–15-year-olds said that they had ever tried abusing solvents, with 1% admitting to doing so regularly. In these regular surveys, solvent use by young people matched cannabis use in 1987–88 but has since remained well below the 10% level.

Source: *Young People and Illegal Drugs in 1999*, Balding J., Schools Health Education Unit, 2000.

During 1998 there were 70 deaths in the UK associated with volatile substance abuse, 33 of them (48%) to young people aged 18 and under. Throughout the 1990s the average age at death has steadily increased and the median in 1998 was 19. The most common place of abuse for adults was their own home, while most fatal abuses by children occurred in a public place.

Source: *Trends in Deaths Associated with Abuse of Volatile Substances 1971–1998*, Department of Public Health Sciences and Toxicology Unit, St George's Hospital Medical School. June 2000.

The links between risky behaviours

A major 1999 survey of school-aged children found a clear relationship between smoking, drinking alcohol and experimentation with drugs: smokers were more likely than non-smokers to drink alcohol, and drinkers were more likely than non-drinkers to smoke. Smokers and those who drank alcohol were more likely than non-smokers and non-drinkers to have tried drugs.

Young people who indulged in one or more of these risky behaviours were more likely to have experienced frequent symptoms of both physical and mental ill health. Injuries were more common among young people who smoked, drank alcohol or had experimented with drugs. Young people who smoked, drank alcohol or who had tried drugs were much more likely to spend time with friends after school. Those who had experimented with drugs were a little less likely to say they were very happy than those who had never tried them, but those who smoked, drank alcohol and, to a lesser extent, tried drugs, were all more likely to have three or more friends than those who did not do these things. (These results were more recently echoed by the research on young heroin users reported above.)

Source: *Young people and health: health behaviour in school-aged children,* Health Education Authority, 1999.

Young people from minority ethnic populations have been found to be less likely to take drugs or drink alcohol than White young people.

Source: *Drug Misuse Declared in 1996: Latest Results from the British Crime Survey,* Ramsay M. and Spiller J., Home Office Research Study no. 172, Home Office, 1997.

Children and young people's sexual health

Under-age sex

A quarter of girls are now estimated to have sex below the age of 16 (ie under age), an increase from 1 in 10 in the 1970s. However, over the same period the number visiting a family planning clinic has increased from 1% to only 8%. One in seven 16 and 17-year-old young women regularly take the contraceptive pill.

The average age of first intercourse is 17. However, young Asians are less likely (24%) to have had sexual intercourse by age 17 than their White (53%) and African-Caribbean (51%) peers. The age at which young people today report their first experience of sexual intimacy is 14 for girls and 13 for boys.

Sources: *Population Trends,* ONS, The Stationery Office, 2000; *The State They're In: Young People in Britain Today,* B McConville, Youth Work Press, 1998.

Teenage pregnancy

(See also the section on teenage parenthood in the Population chapter.)

While the teenage pregnancy rate in the UK is the highest in Europe and is a cause for concern, it has not recently soared, as many believe, and indeed the teenage conception rate is lower now than in the 1970s.

In 1998 there were 44,000 conceptions to under-18s in England and Wales, 8,400 of them to girls aged under 16. This equates to a rate of 47 conceptions per 1,000 population.

In England and in Scotland in 1998, 9 per 1,000 girls aged 13 to 15 conceived before their 16th birthday. In Wales, the rate was 11 per 1,000 population. Across the health regions of England the under 16 conception rate varied from 7 per 1,000 in the Eastern region to 11 per 1,000 in the Northern and Yorkshire, Trent and the West Midlands areas.

Not all these conceptions resulted in a birth: about half the pregnancies to young women aged under 16 resulted in an abortion.

Sources: *Population Trends,* ONS, The Stationery Office, 1999; *Social Inequalities,* ONS, The Stationery Office, 2000.

Disability

Numbers of disabled children

Based on mid-year estimates, in 1998, 393,824 children with disabilities under 16 were living in the UK. Of them, 55,200 were aged under five and 276,064 were aged 5–15. More than 100,000 of these children are severely disabled and have at least two different sorts of significant impairment. This means that about 3% of children in the UK are disabled.

The same methodology shows that 155,976 young people with disabilities aged 16–19 are living in the UK.

Source: *Quality Protects: Disabled Children, Numbers and Categories*, Department of Health, 2000.

Table 7.1: Numbers of children with disabilities by severity and age group, UK.

Severity Category	Children under 5	Children 5 – 15
I	19,872	38,649
II	19,872	71,777
III	2,760	22,085
IV	5,520	11,043
V	2,760	19,324
VI	1,656	38,649
VII	2,760	13,803
VIII		22,085
IX		13,803
X		11,043
Total	**55,200**	**276,064**

Source: *Quality Protects: Disabled Children, Numbers and Categories*, Department of Health, 2000.

Children with significantly impaired vision

The Royal National Institute for the Blind (RNIB) estimates that there were 24,200 children aged under 16 with significantly impaired vision in the UK in 1996, 60% of whom had additional disabilities such as deafness, physical disabilities or learning difficulties which complicate their needs. According to the Department of Health there are more than 700 children aged under 16 in England and Wales with vision impairment of sufficient severity as to be registered as blind or partially sighted.

Source: *10 Things You Should Know About Visual Impairment*, RNIB; Statistics Factsheet, RNIB; *The Specific Health Needs of Children and Young People*, 2nd report of the House of Commons Health Select Committee, 1997.

Children with hearing disabilities

The Royal National Institute for Deaf People (RNID) estimates there to be between 23,000 and 25,000 children (aged 0–15 years) who are permanently deaf or hard of hearing in the UK.

Source: *Statistics on Deafness*, RNID, 1997.

The National Deaf Children's Society (NDCS) estimates that 840 children are born in the UK every year with a significant permanent hearing impairment. Half of all these children will not be diagnosed until they reach the age of 18 months, and a quarter will not be identified as being deaf until they are three and a half years old.

Source: *Statistical Sources of Information on Childhood Deafness*, National Deaf Children's Society.

Recent research concerning the needs of deaf people from minority ethnic groups and their families found that while statutory and voluntary sectors are beginning to respond to the needs of these groups, many barriers to social inclusion still stand in their way. Many minority ethnic deaf people and parents of deaf children were concerned that deaf people found it difficult to learn about their ethnicity and religion. It was felt that schools for deaf children could play a stronger role in the development of a positive ethnic identity. Access to information and services was hampered by poor provision of both community language and sign language interpreters. The mainly hearing minority workers in the statutory sector felt unsupported, often faced racial hostility from White colleagues and users and had limited prospects for career progression.

Source: *Deafness and ethnicity: Services, policy and politics*, Ahmad et al., The Policy Press for the Joseph Rowntree Foundation, 1998.

Cerebral palsy

Cerebral Palsy describes a physical impairment that affects movement. The movement problems vary from the barely noticeable to the extremely severe. One in every 400 babies born in this country has cerebral palsy, 1,500 children every year.

Between a quarter and a third of children and adolescents with cerebral palsy are also affected by epilepsy. People with cerebral palsy often have difficulty controlling their movement and facial expressions but this does not necessarily mean that their mental abilities are in any way impaired. Some are of higher than average intelligence, others have moderate or severe learning difficulties. Most, like most people without cerebral palsy, are of average intelligence.

Source: *What is cerebral palsy?* Scope.

Epilepsy

In 1997, the British Epilepsy Association (BEA) estimated that at least 50,000 children in the UK suffered from epilepsy and that it affected five in every 1,000 children under 11 years of age. It is the most common neurological disorder encountered by general paediatricians and paediatric neurologists, but is often misdiagnosed in children.

Source: *The Specific Health Needs of Children and Young People*, 2nd report of the House of Commons Health Select Committee, 1997.

Autism

The National Autistic Society (NAS) estimate that there are some 73,000 children with autism in the UK. Autism is a pervasive developmental disorder arising from a physical dysfunction of the brain, the cause of which is not yet known. It affects four times as many boys as girls. It spans a spectrum ranging from children with extreme behavioural problems and severe communication difficulties to children with above-average IQs and no actual learning disability, but severe social impairment. This makes diagnosis and therapy difficult.

Source: *The Specific Health Needs of Children and Young People*, 2nd report of the House of Commons Health Select Committee, 1997.

Down's Syndrome

For every 1,000 babies born, one will have Down's Syndrome, and about 1,000 babies are born with Down's Syndrome each year. There are more differences between people with Down's Syndrome than there are similarities. They will have many of their families' distinctive characteristics and will therefore resemble their brothers and sisters. As well as these individual characteristics, they will have physical features shared by others with Down's Syndrome. They will also have a learning disability. However, there is wide variation in mental abilities, behaviour and physical development in individuals with Down's Syndrome.

Source: Down's Syndrome Association, 1998.

The cost of childhood disability

Research carried out in 1997 estimated an average cost of £7,355 a year to bring up a child with a severe disability. This is at least three times more than the amount required to bring up a child without a disability, established in a study using a similar methodology. Benefits for severely disabled children would need to be increased by between 20% and 50%, depending on the child's age and type of impairment, to meet the costs of the minimum essential budgets.

The shortfalls in benefits were based on figures that assume families are receiving the maximum benefits available. This is not always the case; parents participating in the study stressed the difficulties of finding out about and claiming benefits. Most of these families are unable to increase their income through paid employment because of the demands of caring, as well as the lack of suitable childcare.

Source: *Paying to Care: the cost of childhood disability*, by Dobson B. and Middleton S., Joseph Rowntree Foundation, 1998.

What parents of disabled children say they most need and don't get

- Enough money.
- Help planning their child's future.
- Help with the care of their child, both short-term breaks and more help during the school holidays.
- Someone to show them what services are available.
- A chance to learn skills to help their child's development, and to tackle sleep and behavioural problems.
- Someone to talk to about their child.
- More time to spend with their other children and their partner.

Source: *Community Care into Practice* series, The Policy Press/Community Care, 1995.

The needs of families caring for more than one disabled child

Around 17,000 families in the UK have more than one disabled child. Up to 7,500 of them have two or more children with a severe impairment. Their numbers were estimated for the first time in the first stage of this research project and comparisons made with families with one disabled child. This found that families with two or more severely disabled children were more likely to be disadvantaged through not working and because of reliance on benefits, with greater incidence of lone parenthood and parental ill health or impairment.

The second stage of the research project set out to investigate the situation of these families more fully, to find out the particular difficulties they are likely to face, and to identify how agencies can provide appropriate support. The research found that:

- Meeting the needs of two or more children with severe impairments simultaneously presented major difficulties for families and meant that the availability of two carers was crucial, especially at busy family times such as before and after school.
- The importance of having two carers meant that few parents were in a position to work, even though almost all said they would have liked to do so.

- The failure of benefits agencies to recognise the cumulative impact of having two or more severely disabled children meant that financial support was far from adequate for most of these families, who relied on state benefits.
- The whole family was involved in providing care and support – including disabled children and their non-disabled siblings – and the whole family was affected by restrictions on their lives and by feelings of isolation.
- The families valued support that was flexible, was designed around family routines and crises, met the whole family's needs and provided opportunities for a complete break.
- Co-ordinated support and inter-agency working seldom happened, even though families saw it as vital. Families were often in touch with many different agencies and professionals for each child (especially where children had different impairments).

Source: *At the double: Supporting families with two or more severely disabled children*, by Tozer R., Joseph Rowntree Foundation, 1999.

The needs of minority ethnic families caring for a severely disabled child

Research into this issue has found that overall, families from minority ethnic groups caring for a severely disabled child are even more disadvantaged than White families in similar situations.

More specifically:

- Low levels of employment, particularly among mothers, meant that many families were living in difficult circumstances.
- Compared with White families, fewer families were receiving disability benefits. Those receiving benefits were less likely than White families to be awarded the higher rates of Disability Living Allowance (despite both groups having severely disabled children).
- Poor interpreting support and limited availability of translated materials could make access to appropriate information difficult, particularly for Bangladeshi families.
- Indian and Black African/Caribbean families reported least support from their extended family, with levels of support lower than that found among the survey of White families.
- Reported levels of unmet need – both for the children and their parents – were greater than those found in an earlier comparable study of White families. The areas of unmet need identified were money, help planning their child's future, help during school holidays, personal guidance about available services, skills to help the child, a break from care and help with behaviour/sleep problems.

Source: *On the edge: Minority ethnic families caring for a severely disabled child*, Chamba R., Ahmad W., Hirst M., Lawton D. & Beresford B., The Policy Press for The Joseph Rowntree Foundation, 1999.

Improving housing for disabled children and their families

Key practitioners from housing, social services and health authorities were invited to a series of roadshows around the UK to address this issue. The participants agreed:

- Barriers to meeting the housing needs of disabled children and their families are wide-ranging. Issues of national and local policy – in terms of both housing and social service provision, as well as practice – are implicated.
- While resources were identified as a key barrier to ensuring families lived in suitable housing, it was felt that lack of finances are not the only issue.
- The other barriers fell into one of the following broad categories: housing stock and conditions, a lack of awareness of the problems faced by families with disabled children, approaches to disability and childhood, legislative and policy frameworks, service delivery, and ineffective joint working.
- There was consensus that changes in policy and the issuing of joint guidance from the Departments of Health and the Environment, Transport and the Regions were needed to promote and support change nationally.

Source: *Making homes fit for children: working together to promote change in the lives of disabled children*, Beresford B. and Oldman C., Community Care into Practice series by the Policy Press, 2000.

The rights of disabled children

Research has found little evidence of disabled children's 'wishes and feelings' about their placements being 'ascertained', as stipulated by the Children Act 1989.

Source: *Still Missing? Volume 1: The experiences of disabled children and young people living away from their families* and *Still Missing? Volume 2: Disabled Children and the Children Act*, The Who Cares? Trust, 1998.

A recent study by Barnardo's found that:

- Social services tend to adopt a 'medical model' approach to disabled children and fail to tackle the disabling barriers experienced by children with physical, sensory and/or intellectual impairments.
- One of the consequences is that segregated services continue to be used, thus perpetuating disabled children's experiences of being set apart from their local communities, their families and peer group.
- Referrals and assessments do not focus on disabled children's entitlements to support to access leisure, recreational and play activities.
- Resources remain tied up in segregated services rather than being used to help disabled children gain equal access to cultural, artistic, recreational and leisure activities.
- Not enough has been done to enable disabled children to attend local day care services.

- Too many disabled children are still being sent away to residential schools as a way of providing support to their families and this undermines their human right to a family life. Disabled children are more likely to be placed in residential settings than non-disabled children.
- Disabled children and young people are often denied their human right to communicate their views.
- Disabled children are particularly at risk of a failure to respect their human right to be protected from abuse.

The report puts forward four principles which should underpin the relationship between social services and disabled children: entitlement, the social model of disability, a need-led approach, and the promotion of choice.

Source: *Accessing Human Rights – Disabled Children and The Children Act,* Morris J., Barnardo's, 1998.

The views of young black disabled people about independent living

Research with 44 disabled young people of Asian, African and Caribbean origin found that:

- They defined independence as having choice and control in their lives. However, family and cultural expectations sometimes determined how this choice was expressed.

- While there was an association between independent living and living on your own, the young people felt how you lived your life and making decisions was as important as where you lived.
- Most had negative experiences of primary and secondary education and how it had prepared them for adult life. Many felt this was due to professionals' expectations of them being low because of their race, culture and disability.
- Many felt their education concentrated on physical rather than academic needs, so they did not achieve much. Those who went on to further education had more positive experiences.
- Loneliness was an issue for most, particularly for those living alone.
- There was a lack of informal support with little chance for them to meet other young Black disabled people and to share experiences.

Source: *Between ambition and achievement: young black disabled people's views and experiences of independence and independent living,* by Bignall T. and Butt J, The Policy Press, 2000.

Disabled children at residential school

Research into policy and practice in 21 local authorities found that:

- The likelihood of a disabled child being sent to residential school varies greatly across the country.

- Inability to meet a child's educational needs locally and pressure on families were the two main reasons given for a disabled child going to residential school.
- In most authorities, placements funded solely by the education department attracted little or no attention from social services. Most education departments were unaware of their legal duties to notify social services about disabled children going to residential school.
- There was a more general lack of clarity about social service departments' duties towards disabled children at residential school.
- Education departments rarely seek the views of disabled children about how best to meet their needs. Social service departments were more likely to consult with children but they did not always check to see that this was done.

Source: *Disabled children and residential schools: a survey of local authority policy and practice,* by Abbott D., Morris J. and Ward L., Norah Fry Research Centre, University of Bristol, 2000.

(For more information about disabled children and education see the Special Needs section of the Education chapter.)

How disabled people are treated by others

A recent MENCAP survey examined the range and nature of bullying experienced by people with a learning disability and the extent to which it affected the everyday lives of those who experience it.
It found that:

- Nearly 9 out of 10 people with a learning disability (88%) have been bullied in the last year.
- Just under a third (32%) are bullied on a daily or weekly basis.
- Two-thirds (66%) are bullied regularly (more than once a month).
- Nearly half (45%) are being called names in a public place; 29% are threatened and nearly a quarter (21%) report physical attacks.
- To help them deal with the bullying, 70% reported that they needed someone to talk to about the bullying and more than half (58%) that they needed to know who to tell about the bullying. Forty-eight per cent said they needed to know how to make a complaint and 47%, how to report matters to the police.

Bullying can have cumulative and devastating effects. It is humiliating and undermines both the self-confidence of people with a learning disability and their confidence in carers, family and friends. It adds to the feelings of difference and isolation that the majority of people with learning disabilities already experience.

Source: *Living in Fear: The need to combat bullying of people with a learning disability*, MENCAP, 1999.

Young carers

Definition

The Carers National Association defines a young carer as "anyone under the age 18 whose life is in some way restricted because of the need to take responsibility for the care of a person who is ill, has a disability, is experiencing mental distress or is effected by substance use or HIV/AIDS."

Numbers of young carers

There are no official national statistics on the numbers of young carers. Accurate figures are hard to obtain because of the hidden nature of caring, which makes identification difficult. Young carers and their parents are often silent about the extent of caring through fear of separation, guilt, pride and a desire to 'keep it in the family'. Identification of young carers from Black and minority ethnic groups can be even more difficult due to differing racial, cultural and religious needs.

The Carers National Association estimates that there are 15,000–40,000 young carers, based on research by the Health Services Management Unit at Manchester University (1995). Through secondary analysis of the 1985 *General Household Survey*, it is possible to establish that 17% of 16–35-year-olds had caring responsibilities before their sixteenth birthday, and a third of these had been assisting their parents. Of the 1.2 million carers aged 35 and under in 1985, some 212,000 had been providing care since before the age of 16 and, of those, around 68,000 for a parent. A recent ONS survey estimated the total population of young carers to be between 19,000 and 51,000 in 1996. A recent Government report estimates there to be between 20,000 and 50,000 young carers.

Sources: *Where next for research on carers?* G Parker, University of Leicester, 1994; *Young carers and their families*, A Walker, ONS, 1996; *Caring About Carers: A National Strategy for Carers*, Department of Health, 1999.

The profile of young carers

The Carers National Association carried out a major survey of young carers in the UK in 1997. It involved 2,303 young carers who were in contact with 69 projects and also included comparisons with the findings of a similar national survey of young carers, carried out in 1995. The survey provides a profile of young carers in the UK.

Age

The age of young carers ranges from 3 to 18 years. The average age of young people supported by projects is 12.

Gender

Fifty-seven per cent of young carers are girls and 43% are boys. This gender division is more equal than in 1995, when 61% of the sample were girls.

Ethnicity

Eighty-six per cent of the young carers are White European. The largest minority group are Black African and Black Caribbean carers, accounting for 7% of the total.

Family structure

Lone-parent families are over-represented among the families of young carers, although the proportion of young carers in lone-parent families has decreased from 60% in 1995 to 54% in 1997.

Care recipients

As in 1995, the majority of care recipients are mothers (58%), followed by siblings (24%), fathers (13%), and grandparents (4%). There has been a decrease in the incidence of parents as care recipients and an increase in the proportion of siblings receiving care. Twelve per cent of young carers are now caring for more than one person – an increase from 10% in 1995. The vast majority of those living in lone-parent families are caring for mothers (76%), compared with 53% of those living in two-parent families, and are substantially less likely to be caring for siblings. More than one-third of young carers living in two-parent families are caring for siblings (some may be caring for other family members as well).

Nature of illness or disability of care recipient

The majority of young carers (63%) are caring for people with physical health problems, the most commonly occurring single condition being MS. Over a quarter of young carers (29%) are caring for people with mental health problems. Fourteen per cent of carers are caring for people with learning difficulties and this is likely to include caring for a sibling with a learning difficulty. Four per cent are caring for a person with a sensory disability (visual and hearing impairments).

Caring tasks and responsibilities

The majority of young carers are performing domestic tasks like cleaning and meal preparation (72%), over half are doing general tasks (assisting with mobility and giving medications) and a fifth are providing intimate care (washing, showering or toileting), a decrease of only 2% since 1995. Forty-three per cent provide emotional support. Seven per cent are involved in providing child care for siblings.

Services received

Almost half the young carers and their families are in receipt of social work support, the most common service received. A quarter of the young carers and their families had no outside support services other than their contact with the young carers project. This represents an increase since 1995.

Caring roles

A number of key factors have been shown to influence the type and extent of caring roles. These include age, gender, ethnicity, the nature of the illness/disability of the care recipient, family structure, co-residence, power and status, poverty and the receipt of support services.

The likelihood of performing domestic tasks, general and intimate care increases with age. Girls are more likely to be involved in all aspects of care than boys, especially domestic tasks and intimate care.

More carers from minority ethnic communities are caring for members of the extended family (8% compared with 4% of White Europeans); more Black and Asian young carers are girls (61% compared with 54%).

Source: *Young Carers in the United Kingdom: A Profile,* by Dearden C. and Becker S., Carers National Association, 1998.

The implementation of the Carers Act 1995 with respect to young carers

The Carers (Recognition and Services) Act 1995 offers all carers, including young carers, the opportunity to have their needs assessed at the same time as a care recipient is being assessed or re-assessed for community care provision. However, some local authorities continue to view young carers as 'children in need' within the meaning of the Children Act 1989. In some areas their needs may be assessed under either or both pieces of legislation.

Research by the Carers National Association sought to ascertain whether young carers in the UK had received any assessment of their needs under the Carers Act or the Children Act. The survey found:

- Only 11% of the young carers had been assessed (this means that the large majority (89%) had not been assessed at all).
- Forty-three per cent of these had been assessed under the Children Act, 35% were assessed under the Carers Act and 9% under both.
- Young carers under the age of 16 are more likely to be assessed under the Children Act than the Carers Act while over-16s are more likely to receive a carer's assessment.
- Young carers from minority ethnic communities are more likely to be assessed under the Carers Act than the Children Act.
- Most of the young people were satisfied with the outcomes of their assessments. In most cases the outcome was the introduction of, or increase in, existing community care services but in other cases, specific support for the young person or equipment in the home was what was required.

Source: *Young carers in the UK: a profile,* Dearden C. and Becker S., Carers National Association, 1998.

The concealed consequences of caring

Recent work examining the experiences of young carers in the community identified that there are a number of common concealed consequences of caring for the young people involved. These are:

- Influencing family dynamics – when a parent falls ill or is disabled, and subsequently has to be looked after by a young person, the whole dynamic of the parent/child relationship can fundamentally change.
- Social exclusion – for young carers this unfolds in two specific ways: from the behaviour of welfare professionals in contact with them, and as a product of the family circumstances in which they find themselves.
- Substitute parenting – when young carers are in a family with younger brothers or sisters, the complexity of the caring role can significantly increase. In many cases the young carer may not only be involved in acts of direct care, they may also experience a shift in responsibility for the day-to-day welfare of siblings.
- Gender reinforcement – the caring experiences of young women and men, to a large extent, mirror wider social expectations, as well as the day-to-day demands of family life.

Source: *The Concealed Consequences of Caring,* Tatum C. & Tucker S., Youth and Policy, No. 61.

Young carers and bullying

Research by the Princess Royal Trust for Carers has found that most young carers are likely to experience some form of bullying during their school careers. Sixteen per cent of those who took part in the survey were primary carers, of whom 28% were ten years and under. Sixty per cent of the young carers were female and 40% male.

- Overall, 71% of the young carers had been bullied in school.
- Fifty-one per cent were bullied physically and 79% were bullied verbally.
- As a direct result of being bullied, 20% of young carers had missed school.
- Thirty-three per cent believed their teachers were not aware that they were a carer.

Source: *Too much to take on*, The Princess Royal Trust for Carers, 1999.

Longer-term outcomes associated with being a young carer

The key findings of recent research, based on interviews with 60 young carers aged 16–25 are:

- A large proportion of young carers have educational problems and miss school. Many fail to attain qualifications. This, combined with on-going caring responsibilities, excludes some young carers from the labour market.
- Leaving home is problematic for many young carers, particularly if they have a parent who needs considerable help and support.
- Where a parent has a severe and enduring mental health problem, some young people reach crisis point and leave home prematurely, sometimes to be taken into care.

- Young carers mature quickly and gain practical skills that aid independence. However, these gains are easily outweighed by decreased educational, social and employment opportunities.
- Many families receive no or inadequate social care services. Where services are provided they are sometimes inappropriate, intrusive or too costly.
- Services need to focus on the whole family and be quick to respond to the needs of disabled and ill parents if their children are to be prevented from taking on inappropriate caring roles, and from suffering the attendant problems in managing their own transitions to adulthood.

Source: *Growing up Caring: Vulnerability and Transition to Adulthood – Young Carers' Experiences*, National Youth Agency, 2000.

A report by The Children's Society asked former young carers to identify the short- and longer-term impact of caring. It found the following:

Health and well-being

- About 28% of the former carers felt their physical health had suffered as a result of the time they had spent caring. The physical health of a number of former young carers continued to be affected long after direct caring had ceased. Backache caused by lifting, weight loss, allergies and ulcers were among the on-going illnesses and incapacities.
- Forty per cent of the former young carers thought their mental health had been directly affected. Emotional traumas, depression, stress and low self-esteem were not uncommon.

- Seventy per cent revealed long-term psychological effects. This was evident especially where the person in need of care had alcohol or mental health problems.
- Fifty per cent had (or were still having) some form of counselling, or were considering counselling because the stresses of their caring years had left unresolved needs.

Impact on life chances and opportunities

- Over 70% felt that their education had been affected by their caring responsibilities. In a number of instances school was remembered as a painful social experience. Memories involving feelings of isolation, frustration and depression still persisted.
- Some former young carers had returned to education at a later stage in their lives to pursue the qualifications they had been unable to gain, or to study for occupational and vocational qualifications.
- In many cases being a young carer influenced later career choices and aspirations. Almost 50% attributed their chosen career in a caring profession to caring experiences and the acquisition of skills that they felt confident to use.

Source: *On small shoulders: learning from the experiences of former young carers*, Frank J. et al., The Children's Society, 1999.

Children and young people who offend

Crime rates

In 1998, 532,000 people were found guilty or cautioned for an indictable offence in England and Wales, about 7% more than in 1997. The vast majority of these convicted offenders, 82%, were male. For both males and females, it is young adults who offend the most. In 1998, 674 per 10,000 population of men aged 16 to 24 were found guilty of, or cautioned for, an indictable offence, compared with a rate of 131 per 10,000 women in the same age group. For each offence group, men aged 16 to 24 were the most likely to have committed an offence.

Police and court figures show that the peak age of offending for males in England and Wales was 18 in 1997–98. Nine per cent of 18-year-old males were found guilty of or cautioned for an indictable offence in that year. For females, rates of offending were lower and the peak age was younger at 15. Two per cent of 15-year-old females offended in 1997–98. The peak offending age for young men has risen from 15 in 1986, while for young women it has fluctuated between 14 and 15 over recent years.

Source: Home Office analysis reported in *Social Trends 30*, ONS, The Stationery Office, 2000.

Numbers of young people convicted of or cautioned for indictable offences

(Note: The age groups the Home Office uses to classify juvenile offenders have changed this year so comparisons with previous annual figures are not straightforward. Instead of dividing under-18s into two groups, 10–13 and 14–17, there are now three age groups: 10–11, 12–14 and 15–17.)

In 1998, 127,900 young people aged under 18 were convicted of or cautioned for indictable offences in England and Wales. Of them, 99,000 were male and 28,900 female. These figures represent a small increase from the previous year: in 1997 120,100 under-18s were cautioned or found guilty of indictable offences, 95,700 young men and 24,400 young women. In 1998, 58,900 young people aged 18 to 20 were convicted of or cautioned for an indictable offence, 51,800 of them young men and 7,100 of them young women.

Source: *Criminal Statistics, England and Wales, 1998,* Home Office, The Stationery Office, 1999.

Table 9.1: Juvenile offenders found guilty at all courts or cautioned, by type of offence, gender and age group, England and Wales, 1998.

	Number of offenders, thousands					
Age	10–11		12–14		15–17	
Gender	M	F	M	F	M	F
Indictable offences						
Violence against the person	0.3	0.1	3.2	1.2	8.7	2.1
Sexual offences	0.0[1]	–	0.4	0.0	0.6	0.0
Burglary	0.8	0.1	4.4	0.4	9.0	0.5
Robbery	0.1	0.0	0.6	0.1	1.7	0.2
Theft and handling stolen goods	2.8	0.9	15.4	9.1	27.6	10.1
Fraud and forgery	0.0	0.0	0.3	0.2	1.4	0.6
Criminal damage	0.3	0.0	1.3	0.1	2.0	0.3
Drug offences	0.0	0.0	1.1	0.1	11.6	0.9
Other (ex. motoring)	0.0	0.0	0.7	0.1	4.2	0.7
Motoring offences[2]	–	–	0.0	0.0	0.4	0.0
Total	**4.5**	**1.1**	**27.3**	**11.4**	**67.2**	**15.4**

1 – in table means none, 0 means less than 500 or than 0.5%.

2 Offenders found guilty only. Motoring offences may attract written warnings.

Source: *Criminal Statistics, England and Wales, 1998,* Home Office, The Stationery Office, 1999.

Offences committed by juveniles

In 1998, the offences for which most young people aged under 18 were convicted or cautioned were (in descending order): theft and handling stolen goods, violence against the person, burglary and drugs offences. In comparison, in 1997 more young people were convicted for burglary than for offences of violence.

Source: *Criminal Statistics, England and Wales 1998,* Home Office, The Stationery Office, 1999.

International comparative research has found a sharper rise in violence by young women in the UK in recent years, than in ten other European countries.

Source: *Bringing Britain Together: A National Strategy for Neighbourhood Renewal,* Social Exclusion Unit, The Stationery Office, 1998.

Cautions

A police caution is a formal warning, given orally by a senior police officer, to a person who admits to having committed a criminal offence which could have led to a prosecution. Cautioning gives a range of less serious offenders a chance to reform without obtaining a criminal record and many such offenders are not subsequently convicted in court.

The cautioning rate for males (as a proportion of all those cautioned or sentenced) aged 10 to 11 in 1998 was 91%, a decrease from 96% in 1993. The cautioning rate for females aged 10 to 11 was 97%, representing a small fall in comparison with previous years.

The cautioning rate for males aged 12 to 14 fell by 2% to 72% in 1998. This compares with a rate of 83% in 1993. The cautioning rate for 12 to 14-year-old females was 88% in 1998, continuing a fall from 95% in 1993.

In 1998, the cautioning rate for 15 to 17-year-old males was 48%, down 1% from the previous year. This follows a sharper decline from 59% in 1993 to 50% in 1996. The cautioning rate for 15 to 17-year-old females in 1998 was 67%. This continued a fall from 80% in 1993 and 68% in 1997.

The Crime and Disorder Act 1998 will remove the use of cautions for young people under 18 and replace them with reprimands and final warnings. Piloting of reprimands and final warnings began in seven areas from the end of September 1998.

Source: *Criminal Statistics, England and Wales 1998*, Home Office, The Stationery Office, 1999.

Sentences

- In 1998, 49,600 juveniles aged under 18 were sentenced for indictable offences, compared with 43,600 in 1997, a 7% increase. The rise occurred across all three age groups.
- The number of males aged 10 to 11 who were sentenced for indictable offences in 1998 was 390, a rise of just over 100 on the previous year and exactly the same figure as was recorded a decade earlier, in 1988. The number sentenced fell to 209 in 1993 before rising again to its current level. It is

thought that informal action and also the reclassification of certain offences as summary (less serious) has affected these figures over the years.

- Of the 10–11-year-old males sentenced in 1998, 61% received a discharge, 24% a supervision order and 11% an attendance centre order. These figures are similar to those in 1997.
- Twenty-nine females aged 10 to 11 were sentenced for indictable offences in 1998. Of these, 21 received a discharge.
- In 1998, 7,700 males aged 12 to 14 were sentenced for indictable offences, an increase of 13% from 1997. Previously, the number sentenced had decreased from 8,100 in 1988 to 4,200 in 1992. The use of the discharge for males in this age group has varied little over the last decade and stood at 42% in 1998. Forty-nine per cent were given a community sentence and 5% a fine in 1998, reflecting little change since 1993.
- 1,300 females aged 12 to 14 were sentenced for indictable offences in 1998. This figure increased from 600 to 700 in the early 1990s, to 1,000 from 1994 to 1997. Over half those sentenced in this group received a discharge in 1998. This proportion has fallen from 60–64% in the early 1990s.
- In 1998, 35,000 males aged 15 to 17 were sentenced for indictable offences, a rise of 4% from 1997. This continues a rise from a low of 26,200 in 1993, which occurred after a fall from

48,700 in 1988. These earlier falls are thought to have resulted from greater use of informal action and from the reclassification of offences.

- For the young men sentenced in this age group, a discharge remains the most common single disposal – 26% of those sentenced in 1998 were discharged. Fines accounted for 13% of sentences in 1998, continuing a period of stability after sharp falls from 31% in 1988 to 12% in 1993. Community sentences have consistently made up 42–43% of sentences for this group since 1993, after rising from a low of 34% in 1989.
- 5,600 15 to 17-year-old males were sentenced to immediate custody for an indictable offence, including 500 sentenced under section 53 of the Children and Young Persons Act 1933 (also see Table 9.3 below). The use of immediate custody fell from 15% of sentences in 1988 to 10% in 1990, but has since recovered back to the level of 15% for the last three years.
- The number of females aged 15 to 17 who were sentenced for indictable offences in 1998 increased by 500 from the previous year, to 5,100. This continues a rise from a low of 3,100 in 1994. Two-fifths of those sentenced in 1998 received a discharge, compared with a high of 53% in 1992. A further two-fifths were given community sentences – this proportion has steadily increased from 26% in 1988. The proportion sentenced to custody remained at 6%, compared with 2% between 1989 and 1992.

Source: *Criminal Statistics, England and Wales 1998*, Home Office, The Stationery Office 1999.

Table 9.2: Juveniles sentenced, 1998, England and Wales.

	Percentages					
Age	10–11		12–14		15–17	
Gender	M	F	M	F	M	F
Total sentenced or cautioned (thousands)	**4.5**	**1.1**	**27.4**	**11.4**	**67.1**	**15.4**
Cautions	91	97	72	88	48	67
Absolute or condition discharge	5	2	12	6	14	14
Fine	0	0	2	1	7	3
Probation or supervision order	2	0	9	3	11	10
Community service order	*	*	*	*	4	1
Attendance centre order	1	0	5	1	5	2
Combination order	*	*	*	*	2	1
Curfew order	–	–	0	0	0	0
s53 CYPA 1933 order	0	–	0	0	1	0
Secure training order	*	*	0	0	*	*
Young offender institution	*	*	*	*	8	*
Total dealt with	0	–	0	0	1	1
Total immediate custody	0	–	1	0	8	2
Total community sentences	3	1	14	4	22	13

Note: * in the table means 'not applicable', – in table means none, 0 means less than 500 or than 0.5%.

Source: *Criminal Statistics, England and Wales 1998*, Home Office, The Stationery Office, 1999.

Section 53 disposals

Grave crimes such as murder, manslaughter or other violent offences against the person are very rarely committed by juveniles. The fact that such crimes are exceptional is highlighted by the separate legislation that exists to deal with them – section 53 of the 1933 Children and Young Persons Act (CYPA).

Table 9.3: Young people sentenced under section 53 of the Children and Young Persons Act 1933 by offence group, England and Wales 1998.

	Number of persons					
Offence group	1993	1994	1995	1996	1997	1998
Section 53/1	24	16	10	26	26	10
Section 53/2						
Violence against the person	60	69	67	97	104	98
Sexual offences	20	22	39	51	56	45
Burglary	52	51	54	101	128	133
Robbery	137	191	192	275	345	241
Theft and handling stolen goods	1	5	6	10	17	18
Criminal damage	24	23	18	33	32	20
Drug offences	4	7	5	13	18	23
Other	17	19	10	29	22	15
All offences	315	387	391	609	722	593
Total sentenced to Section 53	**329**	**403**	**401**	**635**	**748**	**603**

Note: Under the Criminal Justice Act 1991, the arrangements for imposing longer sentences under section 53 of the Children and Young Persons Act 1933 also applied to 17-year-olds from 1 October 1992.

Source: *Criminal Statistics, England and Wales 1998*, Home Office, The Stationery Office, 1999.

The prison population

(Note: the prison statistics reported here generally refer to 1999, while the criminal statistics reported above mostly referred to 1998. This is due to a delay in the publication of the latter.)

In 1999, there was an average of 64,770 people in prison, down 1% from the previous year, of whom an average 51,690 (about 80%) were sentenced and 12,520 (19%) were held on remand. The small remainder were being held for non-criminal reasons.

Source: *Prison Statistics 1999, England and Wales*, The Stationery Office, 2000.

Young people in prison: an overview

Sentenced young offenders and remand prisoners aged 15 to 20 accounted for 18% of the male prison population overall in 1999 in England and Wales, with an average population of 10,810, of whom 61% (6,560) were held in young offender institutions, 4,100 (38%) in remand centres and 160 (1%) in local prisons. There were an average of 448 young women aged 15 to 20 being held in prison in 1998, 131 of them on remand and 317 after sentence.

In England and Wales the imprisonment rate for young people has risen by about 50% since the early 1990s. Of the 29 states of the Council of Europe, only Romania, Estonia and Lithuania have higher rates of imprisonment than England for young people aged under 21.

Sources: *Prison Statistics 1999, England and Wales*, The Stationery Office, 2000; *Families and Households* by Berthoud R. and Beishon S. and *Income and Standards of Living* by Berthoud R., both in *Ethnic Minorities in Britain: diversity and disadvantage*, by Modood T. et al, PSI, 1997.

Table 9.4: Population of young offenders in prison by sex, age and type of custody, England and Wales, 30 June 1999.

	All custody types	Detention in a young offender institution	S53 CYPA Act 1933 & custody for life	In default of payment of fine	Untried	Convicted but not yet sentenced
All males	**10,816**	**7,048**	**964**	**13**	**1,578**	**1,213**
Aged 15	218	145	29	–	29	15
Aged 16	639	396	88	–	106	49
Aged 17	1,479	736	249	–	285	209
Aged 18	2,090	1,125	307	2	378	278
Aged 19	2,775	1,867	161	5	393	349
Aged 20	2,866	2,078	82	6	387	313
Aged 21	749	701	48	–	–	–
All females	**462**	**300**	**17**	**1**	**76**	**68**
Aged 15	7	7	–	–	–	–
Aged 16	22	22	–	–	–	–
Aged 17	57	32	6	–	13	6
Aged 18	88	45	6	1	20	16
Aged 19	119	76	2	–	18	23
Aged 20	142	91	3	–	25	23
Aged 21	27	27	–	–	–	–

Source: *Prison Statistics 1999, England and Wales*, The Stationery Office, 2000.

The young offender prison population under sentence

In this context, 'young offenders' are those given a custodial sentence when aged under 21 who have not subsequently been reclassified as adults. The total number of sentenced young offenders in Prison Service custody in England and Wales on 30 June 1999 was 8,343. This was a 2% fall on a year earlier, reversing the firm upward trend since 1993. Of these young people, 8,025 were male and 320 female, the latter being the highest figure for young women in prison since 1980.

Of the sentenced young offenders (excluding fine defaulters) in prison, 1,710 were aged 17 years or younger, similar to the position in mid-1998.

In mid-1999, just over 40% of young offenders with immediate custodial sentences were serving sentences of up to 18 months, 31% were serving sentences of 18 months to three years and 28% were serving sentences of longer than three years.

Twenty-seven per cent of male young offenders in the prison population at mid-1999 had been sentenced for burglary, 22% for robbery, 19% for violence against the person and 11% for theft and handling stolen goods.

The main increase over the last decade has been in the proportion serving sentences for robbery (up from 15% to 22%): the proportions for drugs offences have risen but still account for only 6%. Falls have occurred in the proportions sentenced for burglary (from 32% to 27%) and theft and fraud (down from 15% to 11%).

For sentenced males aged 17 and under, the main offence groups were burglary (28%), robbery (26%), violence against the person (16%) and theft and handling stolen goods (13%).

The proportions for females, being based on small numbers, vary considerably from year to year. In mid-1999 violent and sexual offenders accounted for 27% of the sentenced population, with drug offences accounting for 20%.

During 2000, the Howard League for Penal Reform published an analysis showing that the number of girls between 15 and 17 being sent to prison increased by 382% between 1992 and 1998, despite the fact that crime figures for the same group show a fall of 25% for the same period. The rise in young women prisoners, many of whom are mothers, has been blamed on harsher sentencing by the courts, particularly for drugs-related offences.

Sources: *Prison Statistics 1999, England and Wales,* The Stationery Office, 2000; Howard League for Penal Reform, July 2000.

The young offender prison population on remand

The average population of young people aged 15 to 20 in prison on remand in 1999 was 2,930 – 2,799 were males and 131 were females. Overall, this is almost identical to the position in 1998, when there were 2,936 young people in prison, but the total masks diverging trends for young men and women: in 1998 there were more young men being held on remand – 2,818 – but fewer young women – 118.

Source: *Prison Statistics 1999, England and Wales,* The Stationery Office, 2000.

Children and young people in secure accommodation in England and Wales

Secure units are not only for young offenders, whether sentenced or on remand, but for any child or young people being looked after. Specifically, they are provided for children and young people aged up to 18 who:

a have a history of absconding, who are likely to abscond if kept in any other form of local authority accommodation and who are likely to suffer harm if they do abscond; or

b are likely to injure themselves or others if kept in any other form of accommodation; or

c have been sentenced for serious offences under s.53 of the Children and Young Persons Act 1933 (CYPA). As at 31 March 2000:

- There were 441 approved places in secure units in England and 18 in Wales.
- There was a 32% increase in the provision of places in units in England between 31 March 1997 and 1999, and a further 2% increase as at 31 March 2000, as a result of the Secure Accommodation Development Programme.
- Three hundred and sixty-six children and young people were being accommodated in England and 11 in Wales. There has been an increase of 13% in children accommodated in England compared with a year earlier.

- As a result of the increase in provision of places, the occupancy rate of units in England at 31 March 2000 was 83% compared with 75% in 1999.

Source: *Children Accommodated in Secure Units Year Ending 31 March 2000, England and Wales*, Department of Health, 2000.

Reconvictions

Reconviction rates are a key measure of the effectiveness of different sentences and treatment programmes in deterring or rehabilitating offenders. Official statistics show little difference in the reconviction rates for those released from prison and those who serve community sentences. Among young male offenders, 77% were reconvicted within two years and 16% were reconvicted within three months.

Source: Home Office, reported in *Social Trends 30*, ONS, The Stationery Office, 2000.

Characteristics of young male prisoners

The links between social exclusion, experience of childhood abuse and distress and youth offending are clear. On reception into prison:

- Twenty-five per cent of young male prisoners are homeless or living in insecure accommodation.
- Over half under 18 have been looked after or have had contact with social services.
- Over half of the 15–17-year-olds have been excluded from school.

- Nearly two-fifths have no qualifications (80% of 15–17-year-olds), and two-thirds are unemployed on entry to custody.
- Almost two-thirds misuse drugs and a quarter claim current or past drinking problems (three-quarters of whom have never received any help).
- One in six admit to having been abused and 1 in 10 admit to self-harm.
- Nearly a quarter are fathers or expectant fathers.

Source: *Patterns and Outcomes in Child Placement*, Department of Health 1991, reported in *National Strategy for Neighbourhood Renewal: the report of Policy Action Team 12 on young people*, Social Exclusion Unit, The Stationery Office, 2000.

Young offenders and mental health problems

- Ten to twenty per cent of young people involved in criminal activity are thought to have a 'psychiatric disorder'.
- The risk of suicide is particularly high for young people held in custody and on remand within the Prison Service.
- According to The Howard League for Penal Reform, bullying, self-mutilation, attempted suicide and officially sanctioned violence are rife among teenagers in penal institutions.
- Research suggests that young offenders tend to experience mental health problems prior to their offending; a study revealed that more than 90% of

all 10 to 17-year-old violent offenders have been victims of severe childhood trauma and deprivation.

Source: *The Fundamental Facts . . . all the latest facts and figures on mental illness,* The Mental Health Foundation, 1999.

Suicides in prison

In 1999 there were 91 self-inflicted deaths[1] in Prison Service establishments, compared with 83 in 1998. Over the last three years, the rate of self-inflicted deaths per 1,000 prisoners has increased from 1.15 in 1997 to 1.27 in 1998 and 1.4 in 1999. Eleven (12%) of the deaths in 1999 were in young offender establishments.

1 'Self-inflicted' includes deaths where suicide is the probable cause as well as those where there is no doubt.

Source: *Prison Statistics 1999, England and Wales,* The Stationery Office, 2000.

Bullying in prison

More than two-thirds of young male offenders aged 15–22 admitted having come into contact with bullying in prison when surveyed in 1997. One in five said that they had been a victim of bullying and 1 in 10 admitted to bullying others. A self-report study carried out in prisons in England and Wales found that 46% of young offenders had been assaulted, robbed or threatened with violence in the previous month, compared with 30% of adult prisoners.

Source: *Youth Update Crime, Youth Factsheet No.6,* British Youth Council, February 1999.

Race and the criminal justice system

People from minority ethnic communities – particularly Black people – are over-represented throughout the criminal justice system, from stop and search to prison. For example, in England and Wales in 1999:

- Black people were six times more likely to be stopped and searched by the police than White people.
- There were 117 arrests for notifiable offences per 10,000 head of population above ten years old among Black people, compared to 44 among Asian people and 27 among White people.
- Higher proportions of Black and Asian people were remanded before trial, compared with White prisoners.
- Eighty-nine per cent of young Black prisoners were sentenced for over 12 months, compared to 75% of young White and 77% of young Asian prisoners.
- Sixty-three per cent of adult Black prisoners were sentenced to over four years, compared to 58% of Asian and 47% of White prisoners.
- People from minority ethnic communities accounted for 18% of the male prison population and 24% of the female prison population, with Black people alone accounting for 12% of the male and 18% of the female prison population.

There are also differences between ethnic groups in the types of crimes of which people are found guilty. In 1998–99, 91% of those sentenced for burglary were White and 7% were Black, whereas 72% of those sentenced for robbery were White and 23% were Black. Seventy-one per cent of those sentenced for drug offences were White and 19% were Black. More work is needed to understand the reasons behind these differences.

The findings reported above should be considered alongside the outcomes of a 1995 Home Office study of young people in Britain. This found that Black and White 14–25-year-olds were equally likely to have committed an offence (43% and 44% respectively). South Asian young people had significantly lower rates, with 30% of Indians, 28% of Pakistanis and only 13% of Bangladeshis likely to have offended.

Sources: *Statistics on Race and the Criminal Justice System: A Home Office publication under s.95 of the Criminal Justice Act 1991*, Home Office, 1999, reported in *Minority Ethnic Issues in Social Exclusion and Neighbourhood Renewal*, Social Exclusion Unit, 2000; *Youth Update on Crime*, Factsheet No.6, British Youth Council, 1999.

Children and young people as victims of crime

In England and Wales, young people aged 16–24 are more likely to be victimised than any other group. For example, a quarter of all violent crime is committed against young men. England and Wales (together with Holland) have higher rates of victimisation than in 11 other industrialised countries. England and Wales also have the highest rate of fear of crime.

- Twenty-eight per cent of young women aged 20–24 admit being assaulted by a partner at some time, 34% threatened or assaulted. Figures for 16–19-year-olds are 15% and 20% respectively.
- One in six young people aged 14–25 are the victim of a violent offence each year and more than 1 in 3 12–15-year-olds are assaulted each year.
- One or two children die each week as a result of abuse or neglect.
- In 1998–99 in England and Wales there were 26 murders of children aged 5–16 years old, 24 of toddlers aged between one and five, and 45 of babies under one. Of these, only about six or seven a year are killed by a stranger and the numbers are not increasing.

Sources: *Connexions: the best start in life for every young person*, DfEE, 2000; *Taking Risks: an analysis of the risks of homelessness for young people in London*, report to the Safe in the City partnership, by Smith J. and Bruegal I.; *Teenage Pregnancy*, Social Exclusion Unit, The Stationery Office, 1999; *Bridging the Gap: new opportunities for 16–18-year-olds not in education, employment or training*, Social Exclusion Unit, The Stationery Office, 1999; *Criminal Statistics, England and Wales 1998*, Home Office, The Stationery Office, 1999.

Housing

Trends in tenure

In the UK in 1998, more than twice as many households were owner-occupiers as renters – 71% and 29% respectively. Private rented housing formed a small part of the tenure spectrum, 8%. Between 1961 and 1998 the number of owner-occupied dwellings in the UK more than doubled while the number of rented dwellings fell by a sixth. The 'right to buy' is one of the reasons for this trend: by the end of 1998, some 2.3 million council, housing association and new town development corporation houses in Britain had been sold into owner-occupation.

The current rate of home ownership in the UK is just above the EU average: in the Irish Republic, Spain and Greece about 8 in 10 households own their homes, the highest of any EU country, while Germany has about half this proportion.

Different groups in society have different patterns of housing tenure. Those in the professional groupings are much less likely to live in socially rented housing than unskilled manual workers, 1% and 41% respectively. Despite the increases in home ownership over the last 15 years, among the economically active, 9 out of 10 household heads in the professional, employer and manager groups were owner-occupiers in 1998–99, compared with half of those in the unskilled manual group.

Tenure also varies with the life cycle: heads of households aged under 25 are more likely to rent privately than those from other age groups. This reflects the tendency for private renters in furnished accommodation to be young, single and male.

Sources: *Social Inequalities,* ONS, The Stationery Office, 2000; *Social Trends 30*, The Stationery Office, 2000.

Housing, tenure and race

There are differences in tenure across the different ethnic groups in England. Information aggregated from three years of the *Survey of English Housing* shows that three-quarters of households in England headed by someone from the Indian community own their homes. This is slightly higher than the proportion in the White population, about 70%. Only a third of households headed by a member of the Bangladeshi community own their homes. Over half of Bangladeshi households live in socially rented housing. Nearly half of Black Caribbean households live in socially rented accommodation. These differences are likely to be related to differences in area of residence, income and type of household.

Although there has been some improvement since the 1980s, people from minority ethnic communities are more likely to be less satisfied than White people with their homes and to live in poorer quality and less popular types of accommodation, regardless of tenure.

Bangladeshi and African-Caribbean flat dwellers are over-represented in medium to high rise accommodation.

Sources: *ONS analysis of the English House Condition Survey*, DETR 1998, reported in *Social Inequalities*, ONS, The Stationery Office, 2000; *The Fourth National Survey of Ethnic Minorities*, by Lakey J. in *Ethnic Minorities in Britain: diversity and disadvantage*, by Modood T., Berthoud R. et al, PSI, 1997, reported in *Minority Ethnic Issues in Social Exclusion and Neighbourhood Renewal*, Social Exclusion Unit, The Stationery Office, 2000.

Poor housing conditions

Overall, about 14% of households in England are living in 'poor housing', which is an indicator combining unfitness, substantial disrepair and a requirement for essential modernisation. On this definition, private tenants are most likely to be living in poor housing: 3 in 10 privately renting households were living in poor housing in 1996. This compares with just under 1 in 7 of households renting in the social sector and fewer than 1 in 10 of owner-occupiers who have owned their homes for less than 20 years.

Of the 2.7 million households living in poor housing conditions, 750,000 are families with children.

Many Pakistani and Bangladeshi owners live in terraced housing in poor condition.

Sources: *English House Condition Survey*, DETR, 1996, reported in *Social Trends 30*, ONS, The Stationery Office, 2000; *The Fourth National Survey of Ethnic Minorities*, by Lakey J. in *Ethnic Minorities in Britain: diversity and disadvantage*, by Modood T., Berthoud R. et al, PSI, 1997, reported in *Minority Ethnic Issues in Social Exclusion and Neighbourhood Renewal*, Social Exclusion Unit, The Stationery Office, 2000; *Housing and Homelessness in England: the facts*, Shelter, 2000.

Overcrowding

Overall, only 2% of households in the UK are living in overcrowded accommodation as defined by 'the bedroom standard', a comparison of the number of bedrooms available to a household with a calculation of its bedroom requirements. Households living in overcrowded accommodation tend to be those with children: about 8% of lone-parent families were living in overcrowded homes in 1998, as were 4% of couple families with children.

Minority ethnic households are over-represented among the numbers living in overcrowded accommodation: 15% compared with 2% of White households. Forty per cent of Pakistani and Bangladeshi households live in overcrowded conditions, probably because of a lack of availability of houses appropriate for large households and, to a lesser extent, those on lower incomes.

Sources: *Social Inequalities*, ONS, The Stationery Office, 2000; *Social Trends 30*, The Stationery Office, 2000; *The Fourth National Survey of Ethnic Minorities*, by Lakey J. in *Ethnic Minorities in Britain: diversity and disadvantage*, by Modood T., Berthoud R. et al, PSI, 1997, reported in *Minority Ethnic Issues in Social Exclusion and Neighbourhood Renewal*, Social Exclusion Unit, The Stationery Office, 2000.

Housing projections and the supply of social housing

Latest Government estimates suggest an increase of 3.8 million households between 1996 and 2021. Shelter estimates that in the next decade, 85,000 newly formed households each year will be unable to afford a home without help.

There is a shortage of good quality, affordable homes in the UK. In order to meet current and new needs, Shelter estimates that over 100,000 affordable homes will be required each year between 2000 and 2011.

Providing this and tackling the backlog of disrepair in all tenures will cost an additional £1.4 billion of public investment each year over the next decade above the planned level of spending for 2001–02. In 1998–99, 46,500 affordable homes were provided, less than half the number required.

Source: *Housing and Homelessness in England: the facts*, Shelter, 2000.

Housing costs

In the last decade rents paid by council, housing association and private sector tenants have increased rapidly:

- Between 1988–89 and 1998–99 the average weekly rent for council tenants more than doubled, from £19.00 to £42.80.
- From 1989 to 1999 the average weekly rent for housing association tenants more than doubled, from £24.97 to £53.80.
- Between 1990 and 1998–99 the average weekly rent in the private rented sector increased by nearly 85%, from £45 to £83.
- For many people home ownership is not an option. Average house prices rose from £61,000 to £92,000 between 1995 and 1999, an increase of 50%.

Source: *Housing and Homelessness in England: the facts*, Shelter, 2000.

Rent and mortgage arrears

Table 10.1: Households in arrears with mortgage or rent payments: by tenure, 1998–99, England.

	Percentages 1998–99
Owner-occupied	
Less than 3 months in arrears	2
3 to 6 months in arrears	–
Over 6 months in arrears	–
All in arrears	3
Rented from the social sector	
Owing by 2 weeks or more	11
Rented privately	
Owing by 2 weeks or more	5

Source: *Survey of English Housing*, DETR, reported in *Social Trends 30*, ONS, The Stationery Office, 2000.

In 1998–99, 3% of owner-occupiers were in mortgage arrears while, of those who rented from the social sector, 11% were at least two weeks in arrears.

Social rented sector tenants who were most likely to have had arrears were:

- Households with dependent children (31% of couples and 23% of lone parents).
- Households headed by someone aged under 45 (29% of council tenants in arrears and 30% of registered social landlord – RSL – tenants).
- Tenants who were working part-time (34% of council tenants and 38% of RSL tenants).

- Tenants living in London (23% of council tenants and 26% of RSL tenants).

When people fall behind with rent or mortgage payments and are unable to reach an alternative payment arrangement with their landlord or mortgage lender, a county court possession summons may be issued with the view of obtaining a court order. Not all orders result in a possession, but when they do a warrant is issued by the court and may then be executed. The number of warrants issued for properties in England and Wales peaked at 134,000 in 1991: since then it has fluctuated but overall has declined to about 111,000 in 1996. By 1998 it had increased again to 130,000, the highest number since 1991. The number of warrants executed remained fairly steady at about 50,000 between 1993 and 1997, then in 1998 rose by 20%.

In 1999, 30,000 owner-occupiers had their homes repossessed.

Sources: *Survey of English Housing,* DETR, 1999, *Court Service,* 1999, both reported in *Social Trends 30*, ONS, The Stationery Office, 2000; *Housing and Homelessness in England: the facts,* Shelter, 2000.

Paying for housing

In the last two decades housing subsidy has shifted from bricks and mortar investment to personal subsidies, mainly Housing Benefit. As a result, the last decade has seen capital investment in housing decrease by 46% from £5.7 to £3.1 billion. Over the same period, the Housing Benefit bill has increased by 200%.

About 4.3 million households are receiving Housing Benefit to help pay for their housing at an estimated annual cost of about £11 billion (1998–99). However, Government research shows that 90% of private tenants assessed for Housing Benefit reported shortfalls between the Benefit entitlement and their rent. Of these, 70% reported shortfalls of more than £10 a week.

Source: *Housing and Homelessness in England: the facts*, Shelter, 2000.

Rent restrictions for housing benefit

There have been two significant changes to Housing Benefit regulations in recent years of particular relevance to young single people: the Local Reference Rent (LRR) and the Single Room Rent (SRR), both introduced in 1996. The LRR limits Housing Benefit for private rented sector tenants occupying accommodation with a rent above the average level for properties of the same size in their area. The SRR restricts Housing Benefit for most single under 25s without children to the average cost of shared accommodation – or a single room.

Research into the impact of these changes on young people suggests that the introduction of the SRR has made securing accommodation in the private rented sector more difficult for them, giving private landlords another reason for preferring people aged 25 and above. Young people are the type of household least favoured by private landlords and are often regarded as unreliable and noisy.

Source: *The Impact On Young People of the October 1996 Changes to Housing Benefit*, PA Kemp and J Rugg, Centre for Housing Research and Urban Studies, 1998.

These findings are supported by research conducted by the London Research Centre on behalf of the Government. It found that:

- Some landlords had stopped letting to Housing Benefit tenants completely, whilst others had reduced the standard of properties or were using tenants' deposits as a means of making up arrears of the shortfall.
- A few landlords had taken action to repossess property because of non-payment of the shortfall.
- The SRR had caused some landlords to refuse to let to under 25s, whether they were on Housing Benefit or not.

Source: *Housing Benefit and the Private Rented Sector*, DETR, 1999.

Homelessness

Homelessness is the most acute indicator of housing shortage. In 1999 a total of 105,000 households were recognised as homeless by local authorities in England, a very similar figure to the one for 1998. About 3 in 5 of these households contained dependent children and a further 9% contained a pregnant woman.

This figure is only the tip of the iceberg, since, according to Shelter, it excludes most of the 41,000 people estimated to be living in hostels and squats, and the 78,000 couples and lone parents sharing accommodation because they cannot afford to set up home on their own.

People from minority ethnic groups are over represented among homeless households: for example, in 1998, 59% of households accepted as homeless by local authorities in inner London were from minority ethnic communities.

The Government estimates that at June 1999, about 1,600 people were sleeping rough. People from minority ethnic communities comprise about 5% of rough sleepers, but voluntary agencies report that there are disproportionately high numbers of them among the single homeless population living in hostels.

In 1998–99, just over a quarter of all households accepted as homeless in England were in this situation because parents, other relatives or friends were no longer able or willing to accommodate them, particularly young homeless people. A further quarter gave the breakdown of a relationship with a partner as their main reason for the loss of their last settled home.

Sources: *Social Trends 30*, ONS, The Stationery Office, 2000; *Rough Sleeping*, Social Exclusion Unit, The Stationery Office, 1998; *Housing and Homelessness in England: the facts*, Shelter, 2000.

Temporary accommodation

At the end of December 1999, local authorities housed 62,180 homeless households in temporary accommodation. Of these, 8,120 were placed in bed and breakfast (B&B) hotels, approaching double the number in December 1997, but down from the peak of more than 13,000 in 1991. In addition to these homeless households, Shelter research (1997) found that 76,000 people had placed themselves in B&B, because they could not find any suitable alternative accommodation.

At the end of March 2000 there were nearly 32,000 destitute asylum seekers, including families with children, living in different forms of temporary accommodation in London.

Sources: *Statistics of Local Authority Activities under the Homelessness Legislation in England, 4th quarter of 1999*, DETR, 2000; *Housing and Homelessness in England: the facts*, Shelter, 2000.

Youth homelessness

There are no official statistics for youth homelessness, although the Government has recently commissioned research to produce them. Until these are available, the best current estimate of youth homelessness in Britain is 32,000 16–21-year-olds. The way this figure was computed means that it is likely to be a minimum.

- It is estimated that a fifth of 16–24-year-olds will experience homelessness at some point in their lives.
- Youth homelessness has increased substantially since the 1970s. Sixteen and 17-year-olds are disproportionately homeless in the UK, compared with other EU countries.

- Claims for severe hardship payments rose from 1988 to 1996 but have since declined again. However, about 100,000 16 and 17-year-olds claim severe hardship allowance annually.
- Care leavers are hugely over-represented among homeless youth: they are 60 times more likely to be homeless than other young people.
- The number of young people leaving home because of family problems is increasing. Domestic problems, neglect and abuse are prevalent in the childhoods of young people who are homeless; these young people are twice as likely to have such adverse experiences.
- Nearly half of all the young homeless people in London are from Black African, Black Caribbean and other minority ethnic groups.

Source: *Truancy and School Exclusion,* Social Exclusion Unit, The Stationery Office, 1998; *Young People and Drugs,* SCODA and the Children's Legal Centre, 1999; *Patterns and Outcomes in Child Placement,* Department of Health, 1991; *Exclusion from School* by Gilborn D., 1996; *Labour Force Survey 1997–98,* ONS, The Stationery Office, 1998; *New Deal – Fair Deal? Black Young People in the Labour Market,* by Chatrik B., Barnardos/Children's Society/Youth Aid, 1997; *Centrepoint statistics April 1998 – March 1999,* Centrepoint; *Transition to Parenthood* by Kiernan K., London School of Economics, 1995: all reported in *National Strategy for Neighbourhood Renewal: Report of the Policy Action Team 12 on Young People,* Social Exclusion Unit, The Stationery Office, 2000.

It is estimated that approximately a quarter of the 10,000 people who sleep on the streets in England in the course of a year are aged between 18 and 25.

Source: *Rough Sleeping,* Social Exclusion Unit, The Stationery Office, 1998.

Youth homelessness: risk factors

Research has found that:

- Unsurprisingly, young people from the poorest families living in the poorest areas in London are most vulnerable to homelessness.
- Young people who became homeless were twice as likely to have shared a bedroom and twice as likely to have lived in a household with no car than young people from the same area who were not homeless.
- Young people who became homeless had often experienced family disruption at an early age, ie a parent leaving and/or the introduction of a step parent.
- Although both homeless and non–homeless young people report high levels of household friction – 60% and 50% respectively – nearly a quarter of young people who became homeless said arguments frequently involved hitting compared to only 7% of the local group. Forty-five per cent of homeless young people had experienced violence on more than one occasion.
- Homeless young people were twice as likely to report a poor relationship with their mother and tended to have younger mothers.
- More than half of the homeless young people had been excluded from school compared with one-third of local young people.

- This research suggests that it is the most vulnerable and socially excluded young people who become homeless.

Source: *Taking Risks: An analysis of the risks of homelessness for young people in London*, report for the Safe in the City Partnership, Smith J., Staffordshire University and Southbank University, 1998.

The link between school exclusion and homelessness is reinforced in a recent report by Crisis. Based on interviews with 120 people sleeping rough, the report found that more than a quarter of those interviewed had been excluded from school and that 62% had no educational qualifications. The report also found that a third of the young homeless had been in care, that 40% claimed to have suffered violence or abuse, and that more than a third had mental health, drug or alcohol problems.

Source: *Prevention is Better than Cure*, Crisis, 1999.

Homelessness and ill-health

- Young rough sleepers report around twice the number of episodes of ill-health during a year compared with young people who are not homeless.
- Homeless young people are almost three times more likely to experience mental health problems, which are more likely to be of a chronic and severe nature.
- A third of homeless young people have attempted suicide.

- Despite the prevalence of mental health problems, only 22% of young people in the survey had any contact with mental health services.
- Chronic mental illness is associated with females rather than males, with childhood adversity, length of homelessness and with a lack of stability in accommodation when found.

Sources: *Single Homeless People,* Anderson I. et al, DETR, 1993; *Off to a Bad Start,* Mental Health Foundation, 1996.

Research has found that many homeless young people use illicit drugs to keep feelings of depression and anxiety at bay. When drugs become part of a coping strategy the addiction is very difficult to treat. The research focused on homeless people thought to be using drugs, 98% of whom reported that their use had started before they became homeless. This shows the problem of disentangling cause and effect in the context of drugs misuse by homeless young people.

Source: *Drug use among the young homeless: coping through self-medication,* Klee H. and Reid P., *Health*, vol.2, no.2, 1998.

Runaways

(Note: Runaways are under-16s, while the term 'homeless young person' refers to those above this age.)

An estimated 77,000 (1 in 9) 14 and 15-year-olds run away from home each year, of whom about 11,000 stay away for a week or more. It is estimated that 1 in 5 14–15-year-olds spend a night away from home without parental knowledge or permission each year.

Source: *Young People and Crime:* Graham J. and Bowling B., Home Office research study no.145, The Stationery Office, 1995.

Authoritative research about runaways carried out by York University for The Children's Society has found that:

- 100,000 children aged under 16 run away each year in the UK.
- 77,000 of them are running away for the first time but 1 in 8 have run away at least three times.
- A quarter first ran away before the age of 11.
- From the age of 14, girls are twice as likely to run away as boys.
- Seven per cent of runaways are physically or sexually assaulted while away from home.
- In the study, 80% had run away because of family conflict, violence or abuse; 35% identified personal difficulties and 23% problems at school.

- Almost 2 in 3 had stayed in their local area; most of the others went to regional or coastal towns. Very few travelled to London.
- Almost 1 in 10 had stolen to survive while away.
- Most of the young people running from care had begun to run away before entering care.
- Twenty-one per cent of young people living in stepfamilies had run away, compared with 13% of those in lone parent families and 7% living with both birth parents.
- There was no significant difference with respect to income level: young people were as likely to run away from better off as from low income families.

Source: *Still Running*, Stein M. et al, The Children's Society, 1999.

About NCH

NCH's aim is to improve the quality of life for the UK's most vulnerable children and young people. Since 1869, we have tailored our innovative services to meet their needs. We work closely with the children and young people we support, with their families, our staff, supporters, volunteers and partner agencies. Today, NCH runs over 430 projects nationwide, addressing many of the issues highlighted in this edition of *FactFile*.

NCH projects

Type of service	
Family centres	127
Homelessness/Leaving care	55
Residential homes & schools	17
Counselling and mediation	62
Children needing families	11
Sexual abuse treatment	8
Disability/special need	65
Research, Development & Support	18
Community centres	42
Young offenders	19
Young carers	12
Total	436

Correct as at 1 April 2000

NCH employs more than 4,000 staff who work alongside more than 70,000 excluded people. The agency spends four per cent of its total salary budget on training and also encourages the participation and training of volunteers.

Further information is obtainable from the offices below.

Central Office

85 Highbury Park, London N5 1UD
Tel: 020 7704 7000

Chief Executive	Deryk Mead
Director of Operations & Deputy Chief Executive	Maurice Rumbold
Director of Public Policy	Caroline Abrahams
Acting Director of Business Support Services	John Ashelford
Corporate Director	Olwen Haslam
Pastoral Director	Bill Lynn
Director of External Affairs	Tony Manwaring
Director of Human Resources	Janice Cook

Social Work Offices

Thames Anglia

(Berks, Bucks, Herts, Beds, Essex, Suffolk, Norfolk, Cambs, Oxon)
Unit B, Lanwades Business Park, Kentford, Nr Newmarket CB8 7PN
Tel: 01638 751100

London

(33 London boroughs)
22 Lucerne Road, London N5 1TZ
Tel: 020 7704 7070

Midlands

(West Midlands, Northants, Warwicks, Hereford, Worcs. Salop, Staffs, Derbyshire, Notts)
Princess Alice Drive, Chester Rd. North, Sutton Coldfield B73 6RD
Tel: 0121 355 4615

North East

(N Yorks, W Yorks, S Yorks, Humberside, Cleveland, Durham, Tyne & Wear, Northumberland, Lincs)
12 Granby Road, Harrogate, N Yorks. HG1 4ST
Tel: 01423 524286

North West

(Cheshire, Greater Manchester, Merseyside, Lancs, Isle of Man, Cumbria)
39–41 Wilson Patten Street, Warrington, Cheshire WA1 1PG
Tel: 01925 445453

South East

(Surrey, Kent, Sussex, Hants, Isle of Wight)
158 Crawley Road, Roffey, Horsham, W. Sussex RH12 4EU
Tel: 01403 225900

South West

(South Gloucs, Dorset, Somerset, Devon, Cornwall)
Horner Court, 637 Gloucester Road, Horfield,
Bristol BS7 0BJ
Tel: 0117 935 4440

Scotland

17 Newton Place, Glasgow G3 7PY
Tel: 0141 332 4041

Wales

St David's Court, 68a Cowbridge Road East,
Cardiff CF11 9DN
Tel: 029 2022 2127

Addresses and information

Barnardo's
Tanners Lane
Barkingside, Ilford,
Essex IG6 1QG
Tel. 020 8550 8822

Carers National Association
20-25 Glasshouse Yard
London, EC1A 4JS
Tel: 020 7490 8818 (switchboard)
020 7490 8898 (careline)

Centrepoint
Bewlay House,
2 Swallow Place
London W1R 7AA
Tel. 020 7544 5000

Child Poverty Action Group
94 White Lion Street,
London N1
Tel: 020 7837 7979

ChildLine
2nd Floor, Royal Mail Building
Studd Street,
London N1 0QW
Tel: 020 7239 1000
0800 1111 (helpline)

Church Action on Poverty
Central Buildings,
Oldham Street,
Manchester M1 1JT
Tel: 0161 236 9321

Crisis
7 Whitechapel Road,
London E1 1DU
Tel: 020 7377 0489

Mencap
123 Golden Lane
London EC1Y 0RT
Tel: 020 7454 0454

National Children's Bureau
8 Wakley Street,
London EC1V 7QE
Tel: 020 7843 6000

National Council for One Parent Families
255 Kentish Town Road,
London NW5
Tel: 020 7267 1361

NCH
85 Highbury Park
London N5 1UD
Tel: 020 7704 7000

NSPCC
National Centre
42 Curtain Road,
London EC2A 3NH
Tel: 020 7825 2500

RNIB
224 Great Portland Street
London W1N 6AA
Tel: 020 7388 1266

RNID
19–23 Featherstone
Street, London EC1Y 8SL
Tel: 020 7296 8119

SCODA
32–36 Loman Street,
London SE1 0EE
Tel: 020 7928 9500

Scope
6 Market Road
London N7 9PW
Tel: 020 7619 7100

Shelter
88 Old Street,
London EC1
Tel: 020 7505 2000

The Children's Legal Centre
University of Essex,
Wivenhoe Park
Colchester,
Essex CO4 3SQ
Tel. 01206 570109

The Children's Society
Edward Rudolf House
Margery Street,
London WC1
Tel: 020 7837 4299

The Mental Health Foundation
20-21 Cornwall Terrace,
London NW1
Tel: 020 7535 7400

Index